Caught in the Power
of a Thing That Cannot Be Seen

Donna DiMarco

BALBOA.
PRESS
A DIVISION OF HAY HOUSE

Copyright © 2019 Donna DiMarco.

All rights reserved. No part of this book may be used or reproduced by any means, graphic, electronic, or mechanical, including photocopying, recording, taping or by any information storage retrieval system without the written permission of the author except in the case of brief quotations embodied in critical articles and reviews.

Balboa Press books may be ordered through booksellers or by contacting:

Balboa Press
A Division of Hay House
1663 Liberty Drive
Bloomington, IN 47403
www.balboapress.com
1 (877) 407-4847

Because of the dynamic nature of the Internet, any web addresses or links contained in this book may have changed since publication and may no longer be valid. The views expressed in this work are solely those of the author and do not necessarily reflect the views of the publisher, and the publisher hereby disclaims any responsibility for them.

The author of this book does not dispense medical advice or prescribe the use of any technique as a form of treatment for physical, emotional, or medical problems without the advice of a physician, either directly or indirectly. The intent of the author is only to offer information of a general nature to help you in your quest for emotional and spiritual well-being. In the event you use any of the information in this book for yourself, which is your constitutional right, the author and the publisher assume no responsibility for your actions.

Any people depicted in stock imagery provided by Getty Images are models, and such images are being used for illustrative purposes only. Certain stock imagery © Getty Images.

Print information available on the last page.

ISBN: 978-1-9822-1829-4 (sc)
ISBN: 978-1-9822-1831-7 (hc)
ISBN: 978-1-9822-1830-0 (e)

Balboa Press rev. date: 02/13/2019

I dedicate this book to

GOD

for bringing the words through me
and for all the tender ways
he has carried me through all the
days of my life ~

And for

Anthony and Michael

The sweetness of my years ~

Acknowledgements

First I would like to recognize my editor Abigail Wisecarver. Her willingness allowed me to establish an amazing trust. Her performance and passion to help me with my material genuinely touched my heart. My gratitude would pale compared to her efforts.

Also a special thank you goes to the Balboa Press Team which includes Jorge Carson, Mary Oxley, Lyn Mayers and Taylor Kopplin. They all helped to make my book a reality.

That being said, I would like to take a moment to mention Amber Richards. I feel if it were not for Amber I might still be hiding this material. Her unending patience and encouragement every single time I was anxious and in need of a few tender words, allowed me to understand, this woman was genuinely a kind human being. Her counsel somehow gave me a strength I needed and I was able to move forward.

And lastly, to that silent power that lives and works within my skin, I am ever so grateful.

I had not realized when I walked out that door, what it had meant, or even what I was really doing. I only knew I was leaving. I was locking the door on my business and locking the door on my life. I would lock out the past and leave a life of heartache far behind me.

I would, of course, not even know it would be ten whole years before I would come to realize that I was to start a journey, a personal journey of cleansing, of scrubbing my soul and literally stripping my inner environment of any debris, of anything unclean that would slow me or stop me from doing that which would change my inner essence and allow me the privilege of becoming who I actually, really am today.

Yes, it would be ten whole years before I would realize I was simply reinventing my life and creating the brand new me.

As hard as it has been I will say without tears of remorse, without sadness or pain, I can hardly imagine how pleased I am today, with whom I have become. I finally discovered the critical missing part . . . was loving myself.

Today I so much care for the guy next to me, that I am quickly and readily removed from my own needs.

I finally know loving yourself completely is the key component that truly allows you to love someone else, in spite of their short comings, or yours, for that matter. Yet, all to soon, I would come to know that was a gift, and that gift could only come from **GOD**.

I remember one day sitting on my couch with a friend, and stating in my own way as I would then, "I can do anything," that was my line. "I am Donna DiMarco and I can do anything." He would retort "well, what if there were two hundred pounds of cement blocks on the other side of that pond, how would you get them from there to here?" My response unequivocally "I would simply take fifty pounds at a time and carry it across."

Today I would come to know fifty pounds would be too much and in incremental moments and in small loads, I really and truly would and could accomplish all the tasks my power would set before me.

I know too, that influence is my love, the breath that breathes through me, the intelligence that carries me through every moment big and small and again, I am reminded that I call this unseen entity, this vigilant *Power* that watches over me and through me, **GOD**

I want to share some private moments with you. Yes, they came through me, not from me. I will tell . . . as we go.

When you are caught in the Power you will do exactly what has been planned for you. Oh you will think every step of the way, its just happening all on your own, yet somehow, somewhere deep in your core you know, this really . . . is not coming from you.

It could be an extraordinary action and you are so grateful, pleased with your achievement and proud of your success. However, somewhere in your center, in the most delicate and tender crevice of your heart, you understand it is a gift . . . a gift from the power.

On the flipside, oh yes, it could very well be a bad thing, an action you carry out almost against your will. You know without question or doubt, this behavior is not of your character. This happenstance is not within your structure. You lament over this distasteful occurrence.

It happens in spite of yourself . . . when you are *caught in the power*. It is a *gut wrenching* feeling when it is a bad thing. However, when it is a good thing, you are indeed awestruck. If one could even imagine, you feel as though you have been *embraced by* an *angel*.

We live it and love it. We know in our belly it is a part of our human experience, part of a greater portion that sets us here and starts the motion, guides our destination and chisels our path, yes in spite of your fight or flight . . . "You are caught in the Power."

That Power I call GOD! That thing we cannot touch or see, that extraordinary intelligence, that remarkable unknowing source that lives in your interior, that makes its presence known in unheard, subtle notions we cannot quite put our finger on.

It is there! We know it, we feel it, deep in a part of us that will not acknowledge the same subtle murmurs that speak to us in the silence of our hearts and minds and simply allows our soul to live and breathe in this human experience. ***Oh yes, this I call GOD.***

Power
noun, pow·er *often attributive* \ˈpau̇(-ə)r\
:the ability or right to control people or things

There is a madness to our Universe that goes unspoken.
An energy wild with chaos that is instilled in all
of us, there is no getting around it when we say
life comes in cycles . . . Oh Lord, it is so true.

The same idiocy we experience through our most tumultuous
times, is generally the complete opposite of our most
tender and genuine moments, of peace and serenity.

How or why it happens the way it does,
not anyone can really say.
Understand it or not, this is indeed

Divine Order . . .

To my readers:

I take no responsibility for this writing. Why or how it came to me is far beyond my comprehension. Yes, I have written it all, and please believe me . . . this does not mean that I have understood it completely, because to say so, would surely be a falsehood.

Admire the work, in as much as I do and to add, I am most grateful that I was actually chosen to obviously deliver it as such, however, it finally occurred to me that I was simply the delivery boy and that my life examples, for whatever the reason, were being used. With that in mind, it seemed to become a whole lot easier to get this material out there.

My confidence and my courage somehow did not feel so threatened. It seemed as though I did not care if someone liked it, or if in fact, they would not like it at all, so long as they would read the material. I would know the discovery of the words, the ideas so to speak, would manifest in the minds of the readers regardless of their opinion of it. I also knew the power above me wanted it to be as such, and so, it was simply a case of acceptance that I should pursue the journey . . . that would bring me to this moment now.

I do hope that an uncomplicated attitude will assure that this material is saturated within our scope, that people will, in fact, read it and then talk about it. I know that should it happen this way, at least half of the readers will agree with and enjoy the substance of the correspondence.

It has been a great experience for me through the creation of this writing, however, many days and nights were difficult, to say the least. I repeatedly wondered why it was arriving, exactly the way it was. *"We will talk again next week"* drove me crazy, just what did it mean? Surely that alone, was a constant annoyance in my head, and a strong tug on my heart. Nonetheless, I pushed on.

Read it, talk about it, love it, or not, It has been my journey and it is one *I pray you will enjoy with me, as you turn the pages. And as you do, it can only mean this message is in your hands. I thank you for that, but more importantly, I thank GOD.*

Donna ~

Not ever knowing what any of this really meant, I just continued to write what was coming through me. Every page began and ended as it appears below:

Week #
Good morning,
Let's have that cup of coffee together once again!

And ended with:

We will talk again next week and God bless!

Perhaps somehow it will be written this way once again in another text. I am also aware that there were definitely times I felt some of the writing, or more especially, some of the words were repetitious. I could not, however, change the content as I felt so strongly about how the writing was indeed coming through me. This single element compelled me to deliver it to all of you, exactly as it was arriving in my heart and mind.

I also believed at the onset I was actually destined to write a column for the Daily Herald. I am certain I will gain your full understanding of this, as you make your way through this correspondence. I know now though, life will always unfold as it should!

Good morning,

Let's have that cup of coffee together once again!

I had been in the restaurant industry most all of my life. I was born and bred on Taylor Street in Chicago. My father was born in Sicily in a small town called Palermo. Although my mother was also born in Chicago her heritage is of Naples. My grandmother and her siblings were all born there and made their way like most foreigners to the United States and so as a result, I am an Italian woman of both Northern and Southern descent. I feel my Italian heritage has allowed me to become the woman that I am: exciting, strong and to know I have a power greater than myself that functions through me and for this, I am grateful. However, my dad passed on when I was only three, leaving my mother to make her own way. Living in an old Italian neighborhood and coming up hard, pasta was all I knew; it was not before long that I knew my food was my power and it meant everything to me and so, as a little girl my dream began. I knew early on that somehow, someway the world, or at least some of it, would have my food.

For some of you an introduction won't be necessary, however, for many it will. It does not matter though, as I am going to explain anyway and that will be the fun of it all. You see, I love what I do, and when you love what you do, you are automatically successful. That will be one of the most important lessons in all of this. Simply, **doing what you love will power your life**.

I am Donna DiMarco. If you know of me it would be as the lady entrepreneur, business woman and 15 year owner of DiMarco's Restaurant in Antioch, IL. Also for a time, DiMarco's Restaurant of Lake Zurich, IL. Yes, I am the lady that dropped out of life thirteen years ago. Well, not just thirteen years, but thirteen hard, very hard, years ago.

When we are lost, how then do we find our way again? Well, that's what we are going to talk about in this process. I say we, because as I write some of my story for all of you; yes, I will pay attention to my own words. Unquestionably, I will never forget the lessons I have learned in this most difficult time of my life. Understand also . . . **life and mind,** in fact, are one in the same.

So, I say let's have that coffee together again because I sent out a newsletter for most of the years I owned my precious DiMarco's and "**Coffee together**" was my opening line.

Sometimes words cannot say what a heart feels. I can hardly express to all of you what it means to me to have been given this opportunity. It is as though we touch each other once more. Without question it is a gift, however, I know it is not only a gift from my readers, but also a gift from **GOD**. The greater gift is that **GOD** produces the words for me to share.

Well, I must say right here at the onset that what ever I write, type, imply, impart or teach in this material is not documented fact, nor am I or do I claim to be licensed or degreed as such. There was no particular school that I might have attended that helped me with any of what I hope to share with all of you. I guess I cannot be any clearer than that. My school has been the school of life. My lessons have come hard because I have lived them.

I will also make reference in the weeks and months ahead to the special people I so admire and respect and their words and wisdom that have come to bring me to a far more peaceful place in my heart and mind and soul.

So I guess what I am saying here is, that I am only sharing some of my most heart felt thoughts and experiences with all of you. I hope somehow, someway it might help as you travel that road upon your own life journey. So again, these words, thoughts and feelings that I trust we will all benefit from together, are simply for you to accept or reject, nothing more and nothing less and my love is always and only with all of you.

I do want to leave you with this introspection in mind. The seeds you plant will grow. **Your thoughts are your seeds!** I hope to have the ability to impress upon you, the seriousness of wrong thought and how the **power of right thought** will in fact, create a new life for all of us. And please know this is not a difficult process, that as we are born **so too are we equipped with the simple attributes a higher intelligence has so keenly constructed within us.**

"I know of no more encouraging fact than the unquestionable ability of a man to elevate his life by conscious endeavor."

Henry David Thoreau

In our world today, a world filled with heartache and uncertainty, it seems to me it would do us well to seek the change we so deserve. Simply said, I hope together we will all discover a new way to handle the challenges we face.

Having been a product of difficult change, I felt my story might set a powerful example for all of you. However, I am only willing to share some of it as we go along. I have been writing a book for some time and in my tiny prayers, I hope one day to make that writing available. I have always been the first to complain about an author if they were writing a sequel and I was anxiously waiting for its arrival in our book stores, yet, so many authors can even take years to complete their task. So I guess I am average as a writer, or so I hope.

I should also mention that I do realize the memory of **DiMarco's Restaurant** remains in the heart of many people, no doubt that includes mine. I have a plan I have worked on for a very long time and as it unfolds, and if it does . . . I hope to share some of my new ideas with all of you.

Getting back to the spirit of it all, I will set examples as we make reference to life lessons and no question, having locked the door on my 15 year business that was well recognized, I am guessing there could be some of you out there that would like to know why I did what I did.

With that said, I hope you will follow along and that my words will help direct you on your very own path; that some of the answers we are all seeking will be made available through this writing and that somehow, someway they will bring us to a **greater sense of peace.**

🦋 This is a feature based on the premise of love, life and the power of perseverance. Are you feeling lost in your own simple reality? Hang in there with me and I will share with you what I know of "**Divine Order.**"

Yes that's right! With the proper knowledge you will learn a new way and perhaps find a direction that will ignite your soul and surely if not, you can simply enjoy the read.

Has someone pulled the rug right out from under you and you hardly know even how to stand on your own two feet? Well, trust me, I can relate! In a changing world do you scratch your head and wonder where your very next dollar will come from? Oh yeh **GOD**, give me another one.

So in this time we spend together and for the benefit of the help that I might offer, you will learn a little bit about me and a lot about the power you have locked inside of you and what can happen in your life . . . when you come into full awareness of it. Open your **heart** and your **mind** will follow.

In a fast paced world, a world filled with uncertainty, the first clue is **love**. That's right, love. And not just any love, oh no. **The love you have for you**, which is the simple uncut true love that really, really counts.

Unfortunately, when we suffer and many times when that struggle is so tough, we almost pray to die, finding ourselves finally on the other side. Not only do we become better people but also, we have gained and appreciate a new respect for who we are . . . and in that, **that unrecognized love we have for ourselves . . . is born.**

🦋 In the middle of uncertainty, the first clue to wellness truly is demonstrated in the love we have for ourselves. However, we don't start with love. No we do not. Love is at the top of the ladder. We climb a ladder to overcome great difficulty or actually, a mountain. I only liken it to a ladder so I can make reference to which rung you are on in the moment of your disaster or discomfort, whatever you choose to label your crisis.

Yes, that is where I am going with this. You have experienced a crisis. Unfortunately, in our world today, it has all but become a very common denominator. You have taken a fall, you are now simply as low as you can go and when you are that low . . . all you can do is get up. Please allow me to say it like it is . . . **Stand up**, yes, you must stand up once again. Someone once said "falling down is not failing, staying down is." Of course, it is just not that easy and we usually don't just stand right up. That takes time and even though we really don't want to hear it, when we are as low as we can go, there are simple steps to getting better.

Now I know your very first question, if in fact, I got your attention, would probably be *"will this shorten my suffering? can we get through this sooner?"* My answer is quick and easy. **NO. Hello . . . NO!** I am sorry, so very sorry. I wish I could wave a magic wand and heal all of you and myself at the very least; however, there are no miracles. Well, I take that back, there are miracles every step of the way, just no magic to help it happen any sooner than it is suppose to. So, let's pick this apart, tread a new path and see if we can discover a new course.

Baby miracles or life unfolding the way it should be; and if you are living in a healthy joyful place of peace, happiness and abundance, then you are pretty much the best you can be. If so, you probably do not need to read this and that would be my tender wishes for everyone. However, if you find yourself in the same unfortunate and difficult environment so many of us are in at this time . . . I know in my heart I might suggest a better way, for us all. **Miracles really are happening in every moment of your day.**

As you are moving through your catastrophe or again, calamity or "crisis," however you choose to label it, you're desperate. In current society so many people truly are experiencing misfortune. Today I will use my own case example, and so I will set the stage.

Imagine if you will, in a weak moment . . . I locked the door on my Restaurant. Fifteen years I am only used to money, that's how long I owned my business and no matter how tough things were, cash and lots of it, was always in my hand.

Now, I must face the reality along with making the decision to let the business go, there would be more to give up; I was also in love and genuinely wanted to make a life. Please understand, I have had many partners, however, I recall the explicit words of a man, the guy I think I can count on, that said "Let them take this house, give back your car . . . you've got me, let them take it all." Guess what . . . I did just what he said and for the very first time in my life, I trusted someone . . . I trusted him.

Scared to death, I let go of every thing I owned. Well as GOD would have it, sixty days later he left! Yes, that is exactly how it happened. The man that said "You've got me, give it all back" left and when he did, he left me with nine dollars in my pocket and pretty much, no where to go. When I tell you . . . all I could do was **breathe** and **move**, trust me, that was all I could really do.

Devastated and in despair, heartbroken, broke **and alone** (and we will save talking about "being alone" for another case example) I had to keep moving. Oh yes, dying would be easier, but that was not my call. Sure there was that moment, I sat in the garage with my dog (the one single life form, that I knew truly loved me) with the car running and contemplated the thought. No, that would not be the answer. I mean things were pretty tough here, but then again, how would I know what I was stepping into. For sure, I do know this is not my last stop, I believe in life after life, so I just knew . . . I would only have to come back to more if I created my own departure.

In that moment I made a **firm decision** to live, and **firm decisions power our lives.** When you step into a **firm decision** you step into **GOD. GOD** that is in you and **GOD** that is you. *And* **newness is born . . .** *And* **magic happens!**

🦋 There is a knowledge I have locked within my storehouse. That is the space housed somewhere between my belly and my soul, you cannot touch it or feel it, you just know it is there. There in that place, a most unexplainable rousing, allows me to understand how I know . . . what I know.

"The right signs we need to see, the right words we need to hear, the right people we need to be with . . . all come to us in **perfect order.**"

First of all, think about what was going on in your life when your trauma happened. Trace the entirety of your mind and now if I might ask, get a pen and paper and write it all down. In quiet reflection, mull it over and pick it apart. This is called **Examination.**

Now understand some things are going on in spite of you, in other words automatically certain occurrences are happening all the time whether you know it or not, weather you are ready or not and most important, weather you are willing or not. That is called **Divine Order**; I prefer to think of it as **GOD'S Order.**

No definitely and without question I am not selling religion, none of this is about that. My preference though, is to term it as **GOD** you can call it whatever you like. You can say a higher intelligence makes things happen or keeps things moving as you make your way through life. You can call it a higher power, call it consciousness or even call it Kermit the frog, for all I care! Call it anything you choose, but know a movement is happening around you and about you . . . that is right "*about you*" all the time. And when your trauma first happened your **preoccupation with it**, was happening also at the same time . . . in spite of yourself.

> *"The Ultimate Path is without difficulty;*
> *Just avoid picking and choosing."*
>
> The Blue Cliff Record

So now we understand that in the middle of our trauma we are pretty much focused on ourselves. In our struggle we come to know our preoccupation with it, unquestionably is a part of our lesson and also our growth.

Yes, that brings us to the very first rung on that ladder we spoke about, **examination.** This is one small footstep needed to recognize exactly what you are doing. You are looking at you and no doubt wondering, "How the heck did this happen to me." You cannot get it out of your brain. You dwell and ponder and surely are totally saturated with your own negative thoughts about your situation and **YOURSELF!** And that is ok. Yes, thinking about you is ok. We, however, really don't think so; we think we have gone mad! You see in the beginning of *"your crisis"* you think being focused on you is the wrong thing.

You attach that to all the inappropriate teachings you have learned. You have been well educated through your parents, your teachers, your religious leaders and the people, oh **GOD**, and this is the worst . . . that are running your country. They will preach *"thinking about you"* is selfish or inconsiderate or even conceit.

I must add here also, they, no different than you and I, are victims of there own teachers and peers. It has been the way of the world. Their parents and the like never meant to bring about a wrong knowledge nor did ours; however, nonetheless it has been so. Today is a new day and a new instruction is our **reward**. Please, please heed the call, pay attention. There is a new way; a better way for you and for all of us and it is the way it should have always been.

In the end of *"your crisis"* when life resumes a joyful state once again, when once more some sort of normalcy is upon you, **you** come to know being focused on **you** . . . is not a bad thing, but in fact it is the best thing. As you come into this place a special feeling comes over you, it is not all the time, at first, it comes and goes, however, you notice that you like it when it happens. This is **self love** . . . it begins in increments.

🦋 Let us keep our focus on **examination**, however, lets hold it on the back burner as we continue to assess our crisis.

Well, I don't know what your situation was about, however, it does not matter. In any adversity, catastrophe, or calamity . . . circumstances of such a nature, herald a myriad of symptoms and they pretty much all happen the same way.

In my case example we will use **DiMarco's** . . . my restaurant. It is 3:00 in the morning. It is also a Friday; the day has not yet begun. My coolers are full to the brim with food, cooked and uncooked and the like. We are totally prepared for the weekend. I go to bed knowing I have the money I need in my drawer, that the recent steps I have taken will allow me to continue to do business and that, in fact, I have worked hard and once again, I am turning the business around. These were my thoughts as I lay my head on my pillow, however, way deep down so deep an eye cannot see, a different stirring was in my belly.

I knew it all along . . . I knew what I would do . . . I just would not acknowledge the knowing.

There is not even a shred of doubt, not once have I questioned my mind. I just know a higher intelligence, the power I refer to as **GOD**, was working in me that night and I was moved to the moment! I went to bed with one thought. Upon awakening, my plans were changed and they were changed forever. I woke out of my sleep went to **my restaurant and locked the door!**

Yes, I am making a point here. Sometimes your crisis happens at your own hand and sometimes your crisis happens at the hand of another. Remember though, It is the hand of the power you do not see, that makes the final mark in the end. That is called **Divine Order . . .** that is the order in which you truly function yet, you do not acknowledge. It is the gift provided within you, which will benefit your life in so many beautiful ways, if you would only allow it.

Either way, you **are stunned.** The most shocking thing that ever could have happened to you has happened. Oh GOD! What will you do? Where will you turn? How could this be? Please stay with me; this can only get more interesting.

So I spent 15 years in a small town (Antioch, IL) trying to make the business work. The Village, the Police Department and the Masons who owned the building my restaurant was in, did everything they could on a day to day to make my life miserable.

Tons of phone calls and area reporters that wanted a story would move me to bid farewell to my customers. Three months had passed and I had closed and left with no word, it was time to say good bye. A press release was set in motion. With little explanation and in a heartfelt moment, I stated "I did not close over money." Oh wow, these very same folks had a field day with that statement. I had struggled and everybody knew it.

I made a comment with my heart. "I did not care about money." Of course, who would believe that, because I was surely living the part. However, I had started to change over the years I was doing business, no one would know though, as the change was deep within me and I continued to wear the mask. I would be that lady entrepreneur for my outer environment. I can recall different folks would come in and never even ask how I was; instead their first words would be "still driving that Lincoln" and my belly would shiver! Don't get me wrong, money is good and God knows we need it and I am all for that. *And* I still like Lincolns . . . Ok, so let's talk about it.

I am making a point here. This is life; this is the clutter we live in. Without question these are the scenarios we create. We create our own successes and we create our own failures and we do it all simply to participate in our own existence. Why? To discover our truth. The very truth of our existence. ***And* in our day to day action, that reality, is prevailed.** We are here to touch our soul and to come into our own amazing wisdom. To learn who we really are. **To know we are the miracle!** To understand we are not just a human, but **a spirit experiencing our humanness'** for the sole purpose of our growth.

I trust in my heart the creation of this correspondence was to deliver these words. They will sustain you; and more importantly they will provide you with a new way to handle things. This understanding will keep you protected and bring you a new sense of peace. I promise . . . A place of peace within you, you truly have never known.

So this is your reality, your crisis. You cannot change it, try if you might. Think about it. Pick it apart, do whatever it takes . . . ***yet, you cannot change what you did;*** you can only ***breathe*** and ***move.***

🦋 Yes, here we are well into this dialogue. I have stated in my writings previously that **we have a knowledge** of everything that has ever happened, or will ever happen to us. Yes, I believe this to be true. I am here to tell you, we know. We know it all! And the degree of the experience is most definitely irrelevant. It could be a good thing, it could very well be a bad thing and most especially, it could even be life altering; nonetheless the knowledge is there and it is strong!

I also know that as humans we block it, unquestionably we block what we know. In quiet reflection during my most difficult days, I was gifted with enlightenment. I am surely confident that is how these words have made their way to this paper; they must definitely need to be read. Also, please understand . . . I am nobody special.

When an intelligence greater than ourselves has a plan for us and we don't like it, we have an awareness of what's coming.

Many times we block that knowledge because we are not crazy about **GOD'S Plan.** Sometimes, it can even be good and we block that too because, to know would muddle our excitement. Remember we are here to experience, that is what's going on in our everyday earth life. If there were no good things and no bad things, there would be no experience and without experience there can be no existence.

Also in as much as we know it . . . **We cannot change it, try if we might.** We cannot fix it. There is no white-out for life and most especially there is no going back. Perhaps the worst thing ever has happened. Did your lover leave you? Did you lose your job, a house, a car? Could it even have been far worse, a crippling accident or possibly a death that has turned your entire life upside down.

This sounds coarse, however, it does not matter what it was or how it was. We all experience grief and heartache in our own way and I must ask you, or even better we must ask ourselves. **Was there that moment . . . that gut wrenching moment when we knew, we knew that stirring was in our belly,** something not good was about to happen and with all of our might we could not stop it. What is this about? How does it happen? Many times there is an indication, **sometimes though . . . not.**

Yes people are going to tell you, you are making all your choices. I am here to tell you, you are not. Oh for sure, when they think you have made a wrong turn, took the wrong road, did a bad thing, they are going to be the first to stick that knife in and turn it. They might very well be your best friends, your family . . . and the like.

Now trust me on this, they don't mean it. Well sometimes they do. Sometimes people find pleasure in watching other people suffer. Of course, they will never admit that. Sometimes they will say and do things to aggravate or irritate us more. Of course, they will never admit that either.

There will be that moment when your belly shivers or your knees quiver as you realize someone you genuinely love is finding some kind of enjoyment in what has happened to you.

Oh they are all going to tell you that's just not true *"oh you're crazy,"* they will say or *"you're just being negative again."* Yes they will have a lot to say as they try to redirect your life and if you have been listening to the wrong people all along, quite possibly they are in part responsible for what has happened and is happening to you now. Let me be very clear, **please try to understand . . . this is Ego**; their **Ego** stepping up all the while yours is in the basement! Eckhart Tolle expresses it eloquently in "A New Earth" please find time to read the book.

So all of these things make your calamity even more difficult. It is a critical step in the process of growth that we recognize, in fact . . . people, places and things and even their experiences, have a direct effect on our behavior. Ok, so we are not out to blame everyone and everything around us for our misfortune and for sure we will spend more time on **blame.** We are though, simply going to practice a new advantage and create a better way to live.

🦋 I think we will talk a little bit about **DiMarco's** ... There are just way too many great examples in my life story not to use myself.

I want to go all the way back to the year 1989. I was living in Hickory Hills, IL and in fact, just built a brand new home and my marriage was still relatively fresh. Now, I don't know if any of you are aware of the distance between Hickory Hills and Antioch, IL. However, allow me to provide this information ... you could sit on the toll way for a good three hours in heavy traffic and most especially, if there were any sort of construction and there was ... and GOD knows; I did, I did sit there.

Now I need to ask you why any one would want to open a restaurant two or three hours away from there home? Well, trust me, I didn't. However, **GOD** did. Ok please pay attention here, as this is critical to the life lesson I set before you. **GOD did. GOD wins.**

It is so simple yet so difficult for all of us to conceive. There is a rhythm, a flow to life and a higher intelligence has planned your every move. Oh and I know you really don't want to hear this; however, it is a fact. Your life happens exactly the way it is supposed to, in spite of what you might really think about it.

I liken it to a school test, a multiple choice. You are given four options . . . A, B, C and D. Now, you get to pick one and many times you are really not sure, so you give it your best guess. It does not matter though, because the correct answer has already been selected for you. Having great test scores will always get you through school, however, no matter what you do, you are never changing the correct answers. Now, you can fight all the way through or you can accept the right answer and figure out how to make it work to your advantage, in your life.

So wanting to go to Antioch, IL to open **DiMarco's Restaurant** was not exactly my dream. Oh yes, I had a dream of opening my own restaurant. I saw it in my mind for years and when I did not see it, still a silent knowledge, a stirring, so to speak . . . was about me all the time. I really don't quite know how to express this for you, but that I always knew; one day I would be the Lady owner . . . even when that seemed all but impossible.

🦋 I am feeling very peaceful this morning. There is quietness about me, a stillness that cannot be expressed in simple reality. I sit in my silent space and here all things are transparent. The chaos and the noise of the world are gone. In this moment I feel a reverence for something I cannot touch or see or hear. I only know somehow, someway in my awareness this is **GOD**. **GOD** that is in me, **GOD** that carries me through all the times I cannot carry myself.

So many things, so many difficulties in life . . . are out of our control. It is only in these quite and tender moments that we spend within ourselves that we come to our true understanding of who and what we really are. It is a search, a journey through life unfortunately we learn . . . when we struggle. This simple, however, stunning verse is my favorite it precedes chapter one in my book. Please enjoy the words.

"He who learns must suffer and even in our sleep, the pain that cannot forget falls drop by drop upon the heart and in our own despair and against our will, comes wisdom to us by the awful grace of **GOD** *~"* 🦋

Aeschylus ~ Greek Playwright
Agamemnon

∞

🦋 Well if you have followed this material with any sort of regularity, or even if you just peeked in and some of it caught your attention that would probably be, because you might just need the words. Yes, something I have to say here **is being said, just for you.**

You see there are no mistakes, there are no accidents. It is all happening perfectly. It is put together in a most exact manor. It is that perfect sunset when the colors splash the sky. You look up and just know there is something far greater, you cannot deny. Picture in your minds eye (and we will also examine and discuss *the minds eye and how it correlates to your crisis as we move through this self help projection*).

Try to imagine a huge jig saw puzzle; you know the kind we all played with at one time or another as a small child. The pieces are scattered everywhere, not one piece is where it belongs. Now, (I love this part) someone bigger than you says *"put this thing together,*" and they want every single piece back in order. You are young in years and tender of heart, not quite ready to figure this all out. Suddenly, that bigger person puts the entire puzzle back together. You sat forever trying and in an instant, that whole puzzle is perfect. Every piece slipped in, right where it belongs.

Ok, I know you're thinking "Oh Donna you are silly," and yes it is a childlike example. However, in the scheme of things it could not be demonstrated any clearer than this.

GOD alone is your bigger person and the puzzle is your life and the pieces scattered everywhere and your anxiety over putting them back together is . . . **your crisis.** Please stay with me. This simple case in point, will be of such great value through all the days that fill your life.

🦋 Ok lets stay with the words and wisdom about the puzzle pieces. Surely if you read the material you already understand this simplistic example actually delivered a powerful message.

This is probably the strongest link in this entire program and for sure, the toughest requirement **GOD** alone sets before you. The most eloquently said, so profoundly stated, the hardest thing you will ever come to learn in your life and when we get right down to the inner most precious heart of our soul, the song it sings to you is simple, yes very simple. **The puzzle pieces are your life** and you keep trying to fix, to **control** something **you really have no control over!**

Yes, this starts the fight. We surely fight it every step of the way. We don't give up and we don't give in. We will not accept that there is a power bigger than ourselves and for a lack of any verbiage that might describe what I am trying to imply in simple terms, I will say a something, somehow that we cannot see is there for all of us, all of the time and automatically will and does fix every single problem you might ever encounter in this physicality. Ok, so I know exactly what you are thinking right now *"man she is nuts!"* Yes and most definitely your disagreement negates the power of right thought and for sure, keeps the ember of your crisis burning.

I want also to impart here that I am not implying in any sense of the imagination that you do not believe in **GOD!** For sure most of us do, however, that does not mean we trust **GOD** to fix our problems because, for certain . . . we don't. **TRUST** is another issue.

🦋 So I do realize that by now you have probably noticed that with each page I throw out another cue and that I minimize it to almost a single word and then, kind of, leave you hanging. Please know it is in your best interest.

It is said that for anything to really stick in your head you must hear it at least forty times. No, I am not going to write the same things over and over; however, many times for the benefit of the healing some things might bear repeating. For now I am simply setting the stage or sort of giving our process a structure, so to speak.

The **"puzzle pieces"** for sure demand the most attention. I am hoping by now that you are following me with this. The puzzle pieces are **Divine Order.** Divine Order is **GOD.** Ok, nothing can or will change what **GOD** has done. No source, no potion, no magic not man nor beast, not heaven or earth, not the sea or the sky, take all the angels you can muster . . . now, this is where we really need to pay special attention **"Not you or I."** None of this can change what **GOD** has done and what the universe in all of its splendor, has designed specifically for you. You all by yourself are exclusive and what you really are is up for discussion.

You alone are the simple greatest miracle within our existence, created by a substance so genius yet cannot be seen nor touched! A power from above, a brilliance so exquisitely fashioned that it provides a single blade of grass that can even . . . grow a tree.

🦋 There is that unseen space within us all. It is a space so deep, it can not be versed. This is a space only within you. It is so unfathomable, so unimaginable, it can not even be thought, yet it is so immense it can house a universe. Yes as incredible as it sounds, unreal as it seems, the mystery and the magic . . . are all within you.

"You are the creator! You are the genius, the daily maker and the originator."

Deepak Chopra

Please get his audio "Everyday Immortality" take some time to listen with an open mind. It will help you to know, that you all by yourself, do not need a helping hand. The infallible magic that ignites the fire is born in the deepest part of who you are.

There is nothing you cannot do. No catastrophe you cannot overcome. No destination you cannot arrive at. No accomplishment you cannot achieve.

There is no ground so low, you cannot travel. There is no mountain so high, you cannot climb. There is no river, nor ocean so deep, you cannot swim.

You, all by yourself are the day and the night. You are the sun and the moon, the sand on the shore, the flower that sprouts only in spring. You are the voice of the tiny infant's first awareness of life . . . **oh wow, think of it. Truly you are the magnificence. This can only be GOD.** For sure, there are no mistakes, **it is only GOD and without a question you and GOD are the same.**

So go for it. What is it you want . . . ? What can you do with your mind? Think of it . . . and be it.

🦋 I will speak here of a special human being. I have followed his work, his words and his teachings for years. So many times I have read his material and thought to myself "I have written this in my mind" and in our average world, only he might understand that. In his book "Everyday Wisdom" he makes one statement that I love.

"Surrender to a new consciousness, a thought that whispers, "I can do this thing in this moment. I will receive all the help that I need as long as I stay with this intention and go within for assistance."

Dr. Wayne W. Dyer

I fight with the paradox, the reality that life presents to us day by day. They claim and so do I, most times, that we can just do whatever we want. Soar like the angels . . . fly like the birds . . . climb tall buildings with a single leap! Yet, can we really be so sure? How can we know? How can we really know for sure, of this earth life we are dropped into?

I have spoke of the mystery even in this writing . . . it is haunting if you focus on it. The mind boggling obscurity of how and where we come from and how and where it all began. So how can we just be whatever we want to be or is something bigger really handling our problems and or creating them? How does this really all work? *And then* how can you be whatever you want to be if something out there is making your life happen the way . . . it wants it to be?

And now, you are faced with your crisis, the mess you are in. There you sit wondering how did this happen and really thinking "I had nothing to do with this, should I just give up." Trust me I know, I have lived it. Well, I think my rendition of the puzzle pieces is a quick fix as somewhat of an answer, however, we are caught in the middle and responsible to pull through. *And,* then you find yourself again with that same thought ... "I can't fix this, or kind of like, It's just out of my control." It seems like no matter what you do, you are just in a stuck place. *And in truth you are!*

This is the paradox . . . **you can do something about it and you can't.** In those moments though, **you step into your GOD, the GOD within you and a special power begins to emerge.** Yet in truth the paradox goes unexplained and until you get it and know, *you are one with it,* unfortunately the struggle will continue.

🦋 In difficult times there's a thing that I do. I open a favorite book and see if there is a message in the moment. I know the right words come to us and they show up exactly when they are supposed to. You just need to hear them or see them and understand in a faithful timeline, your message is clearly delivered. It could be a movie or perhaps you heard it on the radio, maybe you passed a sign on the road and the words jumped out at you, or you had a dream that was so real you awaken just knowing you should pay attention to the content. How it comes though does not matter, just know the universe, that magic that has created us, the thing we do not see or even more than not, ever give credit to . . . will always serve our needs. We don't even get it, yet so many times it is down to the smallest detail and still, we pay no mind . . . **no heed to GOD!**

Ok, so understand it could be as simple as a button, you lost a button and it is a favorite blouse. Suddenly you remember you had a blouse with that same exact button and it is a top you were going to toss out, it was tattered from worn. "I will never find that old top anyway" you think to yourself; "I don't have a clue what I ever did with it." Two days passes, you are planting, you also have just had a fresh manicure. Dirt is settling in the crevices of your fingers as the thought runs through your mind "where did I put those gardening gloves," rummaging through the drawer you expect to find them in and . . . *"Poof like magic"* to your amazement, you are awed, taken back, there it is . . . the top with the buttons; you never thought you would find. Relief comes over you as you realize you will salvage the favored blouse and then giving absolutely no credit to the power that serves you and without any further contemplation, you shrug the entire incident off, as if it were nothing. **You just had a miracle . . . and don't even know it!**

"Making miracles does not require arrogant confidence. What is needed is a humble recognition that in our uncertainty there is always hope."

"Miracle in Maui"
Paul Pearsall, Ph. D.

🦋 **You!** We are going to concentrate all of our effort on **you** today. Remember this is your crisis and more importantly this is your life. Everything that is going on here is about **you**. It is your body, your heart and your soul. It is your time here in this moment. No one can take it from **you** and no one can change **you**. Only **GOD** and the power within **you**, which is **GOD** alone . . . can and does move **you**!

Once again, I reiterate call it what you like, I like calling it **GOD**. How we label it though, does not matter, no one is keeping score. However, in our smaller mind and let me say here that is in fact, the mind we function with most all of the time, we certainly think someone or something bigger than we can see, **is** really working our score card. I guess it is safe to say this is how most of us average humans view this bigger thing. We're not really sure exactly what it **really is**; however, we just know it is there . . . there within us. Some of us admit it and some of us don't.

Now this is the power point in this correspondence, **it is there and we do know it, in our higher mind** and if we can come into a fuller awareness of it, we can touch and know that part which we truly are. Most surely, we would have a greater capacity of how we function and why.

This would not mean that our crisis would or could be easier, that the bruise would not hurt as badly, of course it does. That is why we are here. **We are here simply to experience and when we get it, when we know and understand that the truth is our ability to experience, and that alone, simply allows our existence . . . it is magic!**

We are the **magic** that is created in the image and likeness of a greater power that cannot be seen. You can read it everywhere today. The books are printed, the knowledge is available, yet most of our society is in denial and will suggest these books are being sold only for money when in fact; they are a gift and a direction for us to discover a new and more peaceful life.

"Do the positive and the negative will take its course."

Goldie ~

I came to meet Goldie through my brothers wife. She is my sister in law's mom. She died many years ago, however, she left a mark on my heart. In her time away from our physical world, she has drawn me to her many times in my weakest moments.

Goldie Jones Christenson was a farmer. As I reflect on the memory, I might have only been 30 years old or there about. Today I am a woman of 72 years, so this is long ago.

They had chickens and cows and rows of apple trees, and in all of natures splendor that small farm was lovely and I would run to it, or so it seemed, every time I was in distress. I could walk the fresh green grass through the trees and feel my sadness melt away as if something magical were happening to me.

Imagine if you might, a woman in the field, a farmer woman, very small, very old. Scrub clothing and a cigarette close enough to her lip that made you think she would burn her mouth. A lovely sun covered face, even then, showed through a lifetime of wrinkles that draped her skin and allowed you to realize . . . **this was an amazing woman of wisdom.**

I can still see her on her knees picking berries and digging in the earth and I would mosey over. "What's the matter Donna?" she would say, as the tears would dance all over my cheeks. Of course, I would then reveal my heart's soul and she would continue her dig, as she listened intently. One special day, I recall how she looked up from under her floppy hat that would keep her protected from the sun, and with beaded eyes looked right into my face and repeated the words . . . that would follow me for a lifetime. "Do the positive and the negative will take its course." The statement was clear and I would retort "What do you mean . . . I don't know, I don't understand." "You do, and you will . . . you just keep doin what your doin cause that is just what you are supposed to do!"

"You will know in time, remember my words." **Somehow in that moment I felt I was talking to GOD, GOD that was in her. The very same GOD that is in every single one of us, and is and always has been . . . just us after all.**

Centered in minds memory a most critical point is revealed in timeless wisdom. There is a power that lies within each one of us and shines through brilliantly and is stated eloquently above all else, that simply occurs, **when we extend love . . . one to another.**

In everything we do, in everywhere we go and with everyone we are with, there are always two energies going on. Yes, there is always a positive, something good that we are giving or even taking from the table. Or something negative that shows itself in the same exact manor. We are either giving to, or taking from the situation; the actual circumstance we are involved in, in that very moment. We can be bad and many times are, or we can be good.

In other words if you can comprehend the level of truth in which I share this correspondence, if you have taken the time to read all, or even some, or any of this writing for that matter, then you already realize and are living in a higher state of awareness. You are in tune with your ability to serve and understand fully that your service here on this planet, is part of a higher intelligence that allows you the opportunity to actually let your ego, come full circle to meet your soul. *And that only happens in situations and circumstances that unfortunately, so many times, really make us crazy!*

Please believe me, that craziness is indeed specific. Oh absolutely. Hear clearly what I demonstrate to you with these words because as time passes and you come into your own amazing wisdom, you can see through all of this physicality and truly understand our experience here. Some bad things happen to give us a chance to be good.

It actually becomes so clear . . . almost like a crystal rain that flawlessly paints a rainbow so brilliant in color it fills our sky and in that we are presented with a knowledge that none of this is by chance; that each word you speak, that each action you take, that each person you help in a positive moment . . . holds a reward for you. Not a reward you can see or touch but a gift within yourself so tender, you can only feel it when you know with a strong certainty you have done the right thing and in that, and only locked inside of you, that feeling is so warm, so incomparable you just know, somehow . . . **you have partnered with GOD!**

So perhaps the incident was minimal, maybe it was just someone you ran into, but they needed a moment to share their problem . . . and you readily took the time to lift their spirit.

Morning turns to night and darkness turns to light and we do not sit in wonder. Unnoticed go the extraordinary occurrences that are happening all around us in most every moment that we breathe.

How can we see a human grow inside another human and not know that we are blessed? How can your vision hold a puppy birth, a turtle hatch, the bee that pollinates a flower, a cocoon that allows a butterfly its wings . . . so many things and we not even turn a head, or give thought to the unseen wonderment that has created us.

You're eyes that can see, a heart that can breathe . . . oh yes, the baby bird that can fly, oh why, oh why he . . . and not I? *And* in all of this we pay no heed!

There is a spirit working through you, an unseen thing that goes unresolved, unrequited, immeasurable, unparalleled, intangible; you cannot view it, you cannot touch it, not taste it or feel it, yet it is there . . . around you and in you, however, most of us function in a state of unreality and convince ourselves we are only this body, this thing with blood and bones!

Suddenly time has passed; life has dealt you a blow, hurled your way a calamity an unforeseen happenstance and you are caught smack in the middle of your crisis and now in tiny moments you begin to notice and **call on a power** you have somewhat put behind everything else.

That power is GOD and GOD will work for you, even when it took your crisis for you to pay attention. Yet, that power will provide your every need and in unspoken moments your heart will swell and you will know, **that power is all there really is . . . . and ever has been . . . and ever will be!**

"There is a GOD within my fundamental nature that carries me. I do not know how, but that it has always been there, there inside of me . . . a swift hard presence the likes of a power so strong it pulls me through this craziness hour by hour, a not human force that knows my inabilities and weaknesses and fixes me all the moments that I breathe. I lean on this intelligence and learn to grow with it. Without it, there could not be me, there could not be Donna. This power is my heart and my soul, my spirit and my mind, my physical body and all the components that make me who and what I am. I call this entity that spirals through my existence day by day, night by night, GOD! GOD in its powerful infamous wisdom has captured my soul and breathes through me and in me and is me and always has been and always will be. My love is for GOD and it is immeasurable . . . It is through this influence that these words, the very words on these pages are written."

Donna DiMarco

The reference above is taken from my life story. It has been a journey. We get here to this place in time and think we are handling life minute by minute, hour by hour all on our own. We are in a constant state of judgment and or condemnation. The chatter in the head goes on and on, not only for ourselves but for everyone around us. We decide how we should be and then, we even decide how they should be. We actually believe all of it is within our very control.

Breathing, the single most critical thing we do is without question, provided by and through a power greater than ourselves, yet we pay no mind to it. The Sun rises and sets for us everyday and we give no heed to the magic of the divinity that is in constant motion . . . for us! Snowflakes fall like Angel feathers and we do not see the beauty, but only take note of the discomfort we must bear. Our eyes are like cameras that endlessly shoot pictures of our world. We don't have to purchase a battery or buy film, we don't even have to press the button, it's just magic and our lens is in perfect working order all the time.

The provisions are endless. How sad to have become crippled, to know the joy it has been, to walk. The Sky and the Sea, the Moon and the Stars are all placed in perfect order . . . for us! **We** are the day and the night. **We** are the moon and the stars. **We** are the magic and the miracle. **We** are the very power that has provided for us and is functioning through us. So why, why does it take our crisis, our heartache and our pain, to realize it?

For certain there is something bigger going on behind the ugly. Without question or query there is a grander reason the adversity has occurred. I can hardly emphasize this enough. What must we go through before we come into reality? How much despair must we consume before we see the real truth in circumstance? And why, why must we bear the brunt of it all? Is this only to bring us to a higher place that would finally allow us to summons an intelligence we cannot touch or see or even feel, when in fact, that extraordinary essence is so readily available from the very onset? And yet . . . even this we know. Could our suffering be eliminated? Would experience not serve our growth and would we not continue to evolve in the same sense of human essence, if this were fact?

A child dies. A family bears the grief. It can only be noted as a most terrible time in the lives of the people left behind. A mother in despair, a father lost in the reality of it all, little ones in tears, not understanding where their sibling has gone, just an incorrigible occurrence! *And* we question GOD! Why GOD? Why?

In our human minds we don't see the larger realism; there is a transparency that all but disconnects the death of the child from the bigger picture.

This husband and wife share a lack of love for themselves and their extended family, which they have actually come to disown through years of petty argument. On the other side of the people that must learn through this catastrophe, there is the ousted family that has been discarded. Now everyone is humble, and humility brings about a new union.

What comes of it all? Well, there is a force that moves within us when we suffer, an unforeseen thing that cannot or ever will be, described in human terms. Many times in moments of unpredicted grief comes a most tender love . . . A love that cannot be compared or even explained in everyday familiar occurrence, because this is not, this is most definitely, not just average bad news. This is heartache and in these times of tender feeling, there is compassion, that force, which goes unmeasured in common hours.

That force, that remarkable unseen thing, that intelligence, **I call GOD; that GOD that carries you through all the rough times, you truly cannot carry yourself!**

I know now your next thought. I know now, you say "well if it is GOD then why can't that power just make it all good?" I say to know good . . . we must know bad.

There is a place inside us all that we somehow arrive at, and suddenly know, things are just not working the way they are. So many times it is a hard call because, for sure, our outer exterior, you know the ego that is playing the role . . . does not want to face what our inner environment knows it must do, usually to find peace within ourselves.

It is most times, when we take the hardest fall that our very ego comes full circle to meet our soul. **Acceptance and the courage finally to change,** come together in an effort to satisfy your life purpose.

I want to say it is a part of a growth we must all experience in this physicality and without question it's usually quite painful. To be somewhat clearer, I would label these situations as coming into our own *"**amazing wisdom**"* which is always most prompted by the makings of our soul, that *inner voice* that calls you to become who you really are.

So in my case it was business and love that pushed me to lock the door on DiMarco's Restaurant. My very own establishment that I built with my heart and worked with a passion. Making my business my whole life because I was simply incapable of being in any relationship with any man and surely not wanting to admit that to myself, would move me to fall. Yes, to make the dive from lady entrepreneur to letting everything I owned go, because that would be the only circumstance that would allow me the tools I needed, to know today who I really am.

That does not mean that I might actually find my prince on his white horse, or that I might handle my next restaurant with any more tolerance when my employees were in fact driving me crazy! These disturbing elements and incidents would eat at me.

However something does change within us. It is the change occurring within the changing moments of our catastrophe and as difficult as it is, that allows us to let go. To move out of any situation that does not serve our inner emotions and we do it with peace and not panic. It does not really matter how it looks on the outside, it only truly matters how it feels on the inside. **This movement of power within us that changes our direction . . . is GOD.** GOD that is in you and GOD that is you, and in this . . . **you are finally free!**

"Looking forward only, unknowing how to turn back."

Sayings of the Masters

🦋 This quick verse brings to mind the difficult stance between power and fear. In fear we cannot look forward. Oh yes, we try to, we want to, yet we are stifled. All the good and right things we need to pursue in our heads don't even come to mind and yet more pathetically only the sour stench of a rotten mania begins a new story in the life of our calamity, catastrophe or whatever we labeled it, which is trapped in our thoughts.

So there we sit wondering why we have fallen and cannot get up. Well, for sure we know why we took the fall. Oh yeh, you're gonna say "this is crazy, and I do not know what I am talking about." You will have a quick response stating, "I don't have a clue how this happened to me!" However, I am here to tell you . . . you do. You do know, and exactly what happened is truly irrelevant to the knowing. Did they repossess your house? Did you come home from work and find your wife in bed with another man, or even worse; was that man your best friend? Oh God, did you lose a child . . . and I know for you to hear this, upsets you the most and I will definitely devote more time just on the "*losing someone you love to a death.*"

So, how can I express for you in one short piece, what I am trying to convey? Well probably I can't. You will just have to follow more closely and I will carry it through, as we read on. I am certain I will want to touch on all examples mentioned, for now though, we are still focused on fear. I want to bring out for you how a thing happens and the specific thoughts that follow and then, how those thoughts actually begin to create a new scenario and, of course, it is created exactly the way we do not want things to be, yet the new agenda begins.

So you opened your bedroom door to find your best friend lying next to your wife.

🦋 I hope you have followed this material with me because I am still focused on the opposition between power and fear.

So, let's take the cheater example. You're taking the stairs two by two, you cannot wait to get in the door to find your wife with open arms, anxiously wanting only you and dinner is on the table. In your head a beautiful evening awaits your arrival. However upon entering . . . a different set of circumstances catches you off guard. You discover the lights are down low, soft music is playing in the background; a sense of romance fills the air. Immediately you know something is not right here. This portrait is not for you.

Instantly a picture comes into your head, you remember the calls you made today. "Honey, I will be home late tonight, I promised Tom I would help him lay that wood floor he wants to install in his new bathroom." Suddenly, a second thought comes into your head. "Tom I am sorry I cannot help you this evening, I have a meeting at the union hall tonight." Then the most troubled memory pushes into your brain . . . and you know! You just know what you will find and more importantly, you have known all along and tried to deny it. You see yourself earlier in the day. You are on the phone with your wife; it is your last check in call till you arrive home tonight. You are running late and forget to mention the switch; she knew you would be late anyway, that you were going to Tom's house. Neither knew, however, your meeting was cancelled.

In a fury you head for the bedroom. You push in the door! You view your wife, there she lie naked, the way you've seen her so many times . . . only this time, laying right next to her is your best friend Tom. You want to kill him, smash his face, beat the air right out of his lungs, but you don't . . . you quietly turn and close the door behind you.

Out on the sidewalk now and in front of your house, you are throwing up. It is uncontrollable vomiting like you have the worse flu ever. Bent over with your face almost to the ground you realize you have allowed this to happen to you, you should have walked out long ago. In an instant the most amazing thought comes into your head.

You,re done. You are done with her. You have made a **firm decision**. In this moment **you step out of fear and into power**.

That power I call GOD. Now . . . your new life begins. 🦋

Still focused on how you have opened your bedroom door, to find your best friend Tom in bed with your wife.

My stance being, we know even the most difficult things that occur in our lives before they ever do and live in a state of denial, blocking the very pain we create all on our own. Surely all of you will say "Hell no that is untrue, if I knew I would never allow this to happen to me." Well, I am here to tell you, you did know and yes . . . you did allow exactly this upheaval to ensue in your life.

Remember last summer's barbeque, you were so involved in the softball game with all of the family men. You knew your wife wanted to leave and surely you noticed Tom near her as often as it seemed possible for him to do so without being obvious, and finally her claiming her tummy was sore and Tom jumping to her aid to drive her home.

Oh God, how many times it has gone through your mind, how many occasions you watched them make eye contact. Over and over you experienced that gut wrenching feeling that spoke to you in silence . . . Leave her now, pack up and go, for sure she will make a fool of you. *"Oh I must be crazy he is my best friend, she is my wife . . . dare I think this way."*

Then the fear thoughts, never ending in your head and for sure it seemed the more you thought it, the more familiar they seemed with each other. Yet you would never admit it to yourself until that very moment, your face was to the cement and you were throwing your guts up.

Oh yes, you thought it and oh yes you were creating exactly what you were thinking. *And* yet we will deny that too . . . and then wonder why life deals us a blow.

"When the world pushes you to your knees, you're in a perfect position to pray."

Rumi

Ok, so we are still in discussion of the antagonistic stance between power and fear and how we allow it to play in our lives. In sadness, in grief, and through our most critical days this most powerful opposition is in steadfast force within our existence.

There are no mistakes. The laws in our universe do exactly what they are supposed to do all of the time, no matter what clutter you create in your simple world. For sure, you have heard this all before, if you touch something hot, you are going to get burned. If on the other hand you touch something cold, you most definitely will catch a chill. These simple yet amazing laws don't change, it has been said, you can throw something up in the air, yet at some point, it is coming down. This is the simple school of life. Yes again, you have heard this before and yes it does bear repeating.

Power is power and will bring forth only strong and rightful occurrences that are powerful . . . In power, we for sure are creating things we want. Fear is fear, try as you might, try as you wish and try as you pray. I don't give one damn how you try, in fear you are weak, you are trifle and when you are trifle you are small, a crumb in the crowd and you do in fact crumble. You just put your tail between your legs and walk away.

Remember as I have expressed for you many times in this writing, I am certain comes through me not from me . . . There is an intelligence greater than yourself that functions through you and is you. We call this intelligence **GOD** and make no mistake when you are acting with **GOD** you are in power . . . **"You are actually empowered"** and when you are as such **you will always and only bring forth the things you really want!**

So now let's recall last week's discussion "the man lying next to your wife in the bed" **your power gives you the courage** the strength and the performance to walk away, not in fear with your tail between your legs, but in strength **with your head held high and knowing this is not what you desire any longer.** Now you call forth the new woman, the woman that is going to love you genuinely . . . with her whole heart and soul forever.

"I have a power. I have a power that is driven in me, a power that is locked deep within myself; with this power I can do anything. With this power I can climb any mountain.

With this power I can sail any sea. With this power I can soar with the eagles and touch the sky. With this power I can feel safe in the hands of GOD."

> I dedicate these written words
> to my grandson, Brandon

Ok this is not pretend, we are not at the theatre, and we are actually living in this experience we reference as reality. In our earth life, this physicality we function in, we are indeed trapped and we are going to live this life every single day. Yes and for sure the words above are not pretend this is highly spiritual thinking. It comes from a source so magnificent, so brilliant, so genius and so completely magical . . . it created you in all of your amazing nature.

I mean really, think about it. Somebody or some thing or somehow we were created. There is a power, a force, a thing we are not allowed to see or even know, that actually made you and I.

Please give it one simple thought and realize whatever it is that made us, that literally placed us on this great earth . . . had to be pretty darn smart. Now I don't know any different than you, was that spirit, a human or perhaps even an ameba . . . who knows? Who cares? **To me though that entity is GOD!**

I say how can a mind not know that a thing we cannot touch or see has placed us here, not ever allowing us to know why, or how we would live or die. Who or what, in fact, is responsible for this amazing performance we star in . . . remains a mystery.

No different than your creator that you are actually, one with, attached to and delivered from, so to is that miraculous power driven deep within you. Without question you will simply accomplish all that you were put here to do. With amazing perseverance you are truly provided with the exact tools you need to tackle your largest and most incredible dreams.

So why fret? Why not put your **faith in the magic you share as one with your power... the power that is only you, the very same power . . . I call GOD!**

🦋 Choice and making the right one can and only, will always push us in the right direction. Oh ok, now for sure I know your thinking this is a huge contradiction to most of what I have projected thus far with this material. Well without question it surely is an opposing fraction to the equation. Yet it is the course in life we must all tread to become whom we are suppose to be, to complete this journey and also to simply fulfill our life purpose. We are placed in this time and space, and this particular container to do a job. You are here on a mission. Yes it is like "Mission Impossible" (if you recall the TV series) and **you are going to be sure . . . it is all possible!** So let's talk about choice and how and why we make them.

And again, I will set a life example. I do believe as I have stated previously "people, places and things, have a direct effect on our behavior" and they come into our lives to do exactly what they are sent to do. I realize this is a powerful statement; nonetheless, it is an overwhelming truth. So in light of this thought, I will attest to a collective consciousness when things go right and even when things go wrong.

So in reality you take the wrong road, make a bad move and everyone points a finger at you. "How dare you do such a thing" they imply, when in fact . . . they were the music that aided the dance all along. *And* so I had a friend. Some people come and go in our lives with just the exact tools to furnish our journey. Now understand . . . that is weather you like it or not. Your life path will find you. What you are supposed to do will present it self . . . and you will leap.

And so I did. Everyday I cried on her shoulder, how I struggled with my business and everyday she would say "close that restaurant." At first I would scream "don't say that to me!" Please know there could be no struggle tough enough for me to close, you can always find money somewhere. Yet there was that quiet convincing that it was something I was supposed to do, not because of money, although, I used it as an excuse the night I cried to her and closed. Nonetheless, I locked the door and left. She said it to me over and over and silently I listened. I am not saying this to tell you to blame, trust me, there is no such thing as blame, we are all just one and we will cover that assessment next. I say this to reiterate the people we are closest to . . . are there for a reason, and the choices we make have everything to do with our environment. It is an extraordinary intelligence that makes certain it is our perfect plan and **it provides everyone and everything** to be sure **we do exactly what we were sent here . . . to do.**

So what is blame and why do we do it? Well, understand the person you are blaming is really just you anyway. Yes, that's right! That person is you experiencing your self as her / or him, either way there is no significance, in both case scenarios that person is really just you. We are all one experiencing ourselves over and over, in so many different ways. You have heard it plenty of times, yet paid no mind at all to a knowledge you have locked within you.

There is an energy connection that runs through all of us, not something you can see or hear, feel or touch, but an element that connects all things to the power that has simply created us and is us. That very same power that has allowed us to be separate pulls us together, through experience and circumstance in unexplainable events that measure a lifetime, your lifetime . . . well lived through a magic you cannot comprehend! **That very magnificence is GOD** experiencing its power through you and is you, and always has been and always will be . . . **just you.**

You yourself are the miracle, the genius, the animated creature placed in this earth life, to be exactly where you are; without question or answer, only to be . . . nothing more and nothing less. Yet we cannot accept that which we really are. Why? Why? Oh why?

The very people we draw to us are the people that will help us to learn our lessons. Yep, we hate them. Most times it is a very stormy relationship and they stay with us like glue and it can even get grueling! Sometimes we almost feel guilty for our thoughts and we even begin to think, something must surely be wrong with us. However, it is not, it is just life, doing what it is suppose to do.

Remember we are here to experience. **We are the product and the purpose** all one in the same, just tripping through it all, unable to follow the road map, the journey we our very selves have created. Yes, we are the unmatched magic . . . the only real magic in this entire electrical universe, the play pen GOD in its infamous wonder, has placed us in.

If a mind can make sense of it . . . in the knowledge of circumstance, there is peace.

So when we come into a fuller awareness and begin to acknowledge that our power is actually there within us, available to accommodate our needs and wanting only and always to direct us on the most desirable path, everything around us both within and without begins to change.

Suddenly you know and realize you actually do have a magic within you. **GOD,** your **GOD** is functioning all the time in your thoughts and actions for whatever it is you so desire.

However, understand what it is that has brought you right to this moment and right to these very words you are reading today with me. Your power your higher consciousness, **that special something that you cannot see or feel**, yet know is there, is always working in your best interest and will only lead you to the path that will serve your higher good.

So you're in the middle of your crisis. Do you think you might have taken a wrong turn to have arrived at this particular destination? Might there have been some performance on your part that could have possibly been somewhat unsuitable or even perhaps slightly inappropriate? Please know, I am not here to judge or imply your circumstance is happening because you were bad.

Remember we started all of this by qualifying sometimes our event or crisis occurs by our own hand and sometimes it occurs by the hand of another. Ok, I am leaving you with this thought . . . sometimes it simply occurs by the hand of **GOD!**

So allow me to inject an effortless yet remarkable suggestion. **Peacefulness is Godliness** and in that, there is no question, however, the pendulum swings both ways when it is about a learning thing. Enlightenment not only comes on the arm of misfortune, agony and despair there is also the hand that includes great joy, enthusiasm and a passion we can only discover in a higher spirit . . . **that is when we gain the true knowledge of inspiration.**

In a world where foreclosures rank at the top of our charts with parents loosing their sons and daughters to senseless wars or any war at all for that matter and with Cancer being the greater conversation in most households because so many people are suffering with it, perhaps, it is time to step back and take a look at what we are doing to ourselves.

Every time you run into someone you know, more than likely they have lost or are loosing their job; these are the situations that are most prevalent in our world today. Crisis, calamity and /or catastrophe have all but become a commonality in the greater scope of things within our humankind, yes and for sure we need to learn some coping strategies. However, the larger reality is that a new way is upon us, heartache and despair grief and sadness can and only will continue until we begin to recognize the challenges set before us today. **It is a changing thing!** As I type I am having a light bulb moment or as Oprah puts it, it is a "WOW" moment!

Please take these words to your soul and know a greater good is available to meet your needs, to handle your struggle, to caress your heart . . . and dry your tears, **when we must change . . . we must grow.** When we do not grow on our own and most times we need the nudge, **GOD** alone steps in to lend a hand. That higher mind, the mind you do not recognize yet, but surely will once you have had to deal with your very own crisis, creates the struggle for you to learn and in doing so, you come to a better and more peaceful understanding of who and what you really are, and finally life becomes beautiful.

On a grander scale and in this time our people must **make the change** . . . I ask you, how much suffering must we bear before we recognize the demand for our attention.? How long before we come into **awareness, accept it . . . and practice a new way?**

We always know our deepest issues and most times they bring us to our greatest fall. We know too, just how to fix it, however, many times our strongest emotions fan from a trauma buried so deep that to come face to face with it, is actually far more grueling than taking the fall.

Learning to surf your way to a new discovery of whom you really are, is simply the easier road to travel, and so we do. We take the fall and block the reality of what made us so successful and how that same, exact ingredient brings us to the lowest level and all in the same mold of being . . . just who we are.

In a step by step process of more than average techniques we then begin to work through old feelings and new circumstances and in doing so, a brand new part of us never experienced before, merges to the forefront.

Now we bare our tender feelings and begin to demonstrate a new personality. We are humble, we have been through hell and back, and we survived. We can get through anything . . . and the only difference now, than from former days, is we know it.

And so in the middle of our crisis and or calamity, our difficulty becomes more than just overwhelming. Our struggle and strife are so tough, that simply getting to the other side anyway we possibly can, makes us realize we are all the better for it. *And in doing so we actually just stick a bandage on the deepest wound, and the most severe trauma imaginable!*

And so it does not take just our calamity, our crisis . . . to heal from the trauma and having to experience pretty much of the same pain and heartache, calls for more than just one single earth life.

Yes, life after life the trauma plays out, one like the other . . . over and over, not identical circumstances, nor the same people. It could be a mother's issue in one lifetime, a daughters issue in another and similar circumstances, yet different scenarios; however, the infection grows . . . until the wound is actually healed.

🦋 And so on the coat tails of all that has been said and having had the courage to introduce you to a new way, I so much hope you will pay homage to all the words that I have written . . . and allow them to bring you into a new awareness of who and what you really are. What will it take for you to honor them? What will it take for you to understand the power within you and then make it benefit all you ever touch, hear or see; oh and if I were simply to try the way of the wicked . . . how easy then, it would become to gain your attention.

Yes, and if only, I could bottle these words, make them eatable, perhaps lace them with sex and murder, would not the entire world partake of the fruit? That is what's going on today. Whatever happened to virtue, to kindness . . . step aside and let the old lady have the seat. Most times in this society and for sure, you can hear it and view it on all of our news stations; after all they are producing what they know their audience wants . . . that same old lady is pushed to the floor and many times far worse!

So one by one, our people are suffering. One by one, they are taking the knocks and blows; one by one, they are riddled with a germ infested society that lives on the wrong side of a consciousness, which is in fact, created only with a purpose to serve its higher good.

So the larger question that looms upon us all surely is and can only be . . . how do we get from where we are, to where we need . . . **and with the help of a higher power are so destined . . . to be?** How much more heartache and despair must we suffer before **we get it?**

> *"Opportunity often comes disguised in the form of misfortune or temporary defeat."*
>
> *Napoleon Hill*

"Action or procrastination" two very powerful energies. What are they really conveying to a mind that thinks? Well for sure we understand one is positive and the other negative.

We desperately want and or need to get something done. We know we have to do it. It is a good thing, well maybe. Maybe, it is a bad thing . . . it does not matter though; it seems we just can not get it together. We just can't seem to complete our task. We have done everything we can possibly do, yet . . . the result we seek has not happened. Darn! We are pretty darn sure we have tried it all, did all the right things, and made all the right moves . . . and nothing.

So let's talk about what generally happens next. Well, I would bet we all know this answer because more than not, it surely is average. We sit on it. We sit on the very thing we need to do . . . or think we are suppose to get done right then and there.

We are not even truly certain what we should do and as a result we feel stuck; stuck in a place we think is not good. Waiting, just waiting, not even sure that what we are waiting for . . . will ever happen. Our perception in our minds is generally "this is my fault there must be something I am not doing, that needs to get done." Most times, as a result we begin to indict our character when in fact; our character has nothing to do with the delay at all. That's right . . . our perception, our plan, the very thing we think we have to do, or actually what we are not doing, has absolutely nothing to do with us at all.

It is an unseen thing, a divine intelligence that measures your step. Oh yes, marks your spot, chisels your path . . . that with which you will walk. *"And you will."* You will for sure walk that path, no matter how hard you try to do it your way. Now, most of you won't accept that, not for one moment, not as long as you breathe in this human condition. You will think you are controlling it all. No, no, no, not . . .You are not; it is the influence you cannot see . . . that magic that tugs at your every move, that power locked inside of you that reaches from the depths of your inner most environment to the crevices of your tender soul . . . *that miracle that propels your very existence . . .* ***I call GOD!***

🦋 You can pick up a book most anywhere, and even by some of my most favorite authors and inspirational writers. You might see that they imply their way is going to make you better, change your life, cure all your ills, bring you new love and help you get rich quick.

Well, do the books help? Absolutely. Do I believe they guide you in the right direction? No question. Could it be that what you are reading right at this very moment might just be what you need to hear? You bet. Now, if at this time you are reading my material or anyone's script for that matter . . . is this going to change you? NO! Definitely no, not even possible.

Only you . . . can change you and only your actions will redirect your world and create a better one if you so choose. Now please understand, that only happens through a power greater than yourself and you must first know that, that power, that mystical magic, this unseen thing that propels your every thought, action and deed, is locked inside of you.

The power you cannot see the influence you cannot touch or feel, that magic within you, decides when and how you will, or will not do anything. That genius... I call GOD!

Your whole world will change. Your heart and soul and mind and body will change only when you truly come to the full understanding that you, you yourself cannot change a thing . . . **unless you first know** a greater ability, a source, a power unmatched in human condition . . . is indeed controlling your every move.

That source is deep within your existence and moves you to carry out the action you need to capture in the moment. It is there for you always and only when you come into the amazing wisdom that to accomplish any task, no matter how large or even how menial you must first turn it over to that power within yourself . . . that power, **I call GOD. GOD that is in you** . . . and **GOD that is you.** *And you can call it Joe if that makes you more comfortable.*

Ok so we talked about the puzzle pieces. We talked about the school test and the right answers. We also talked about, "it not being up to you."

I did not hold back in stating these are not your choices . . . you just think they are. I was even bold in expression, that a higher intelligence has planned your every move. Chartered your very course. I have even reminded you that you can read this in a thousand books and find the material in a multitude of stores.

However, and this is the catch, **it is up to you** to find the right answer. It is your responsibility to find your path and **GOD knows** you might guess for a while, and many times a longer while than we can hardly bear to experience, and for sure . . . in doing so **you will change your reality!**

Just remember while you're guessing, you're stumbling, and in your search you will experience one blow after the other, *till and only*... you make your way to that unquestionable, indisputable and all knowing "**right answer.**"

Yes and in that certainty, which is in fact the journey of a lifetime . . . your life; then and only then will you come face to face with that unseen power, that most unbelievable, inconceivable intelligence that has carried you through every moment, while you thought all the way, you were doing it . . . **all on your own!**

In this lies the miracle of GOD. Where will it take you? How do we know? The answer is locked deep within your center. Every heart within our universe holds a message, so to does yours . . . designed specifically for you. Therein lives the power of an unseen thing . . . *And* **this nameless appreciative can only be GOD.**

🦋 I had let go of everything. In my distress I could not even imagine what I would do, where I would turn. No one was there; no one was there with me . . . How could that be?

How could it be that all those people that were there, when I was that special lady entrepreneur . . . were just gone, when I needed them?

Well, as GOD would have it, I was on a journey. Yes, I was out to touch my soul. I didn't know that though, not yet. I thought I was going to find that little girl inside of me that wanted to win the world; instead I found my spirit . . . that place of peace where we can only know a higher power.

I had lost everything but I had found myself. I was in a tiny three room apartment, the cutest smallest place I had ever lived in . . . and I was more peaceful . . . than I had ever been in my life.

You see, you cannot get there; you cannot get to that place with a bunch of people helping you along and making things easy for you. You cannot really touch your soul until you find that incredible, unquestionable, love and true respect, you have for yourself. "That's right for you."

It almost compares, yet still pales to the inextricable love you realize when you finally come to know **GOD** . . . To finally know that there is only **GOD** . . . that there has only been, *and that there will always and only be, "that power." That spirit spot within you always has . . . and will continue, to carry you through anything!*

That is the magic...

🦋 It is said there is a thread that connects us. It is said, there is an unforeseen thing that bounds us together, that ties us to each other and to all things . . . we are one.

So why? Why is it that we treat each other so poorly? Why is it so many times the ones we love the very most, we kick the hardest? What is it within us that allow us to take for granted the very sweetest gifts GOD alone has provided, of course, that is the people we love and cherish. Yet . . . we push them aside like they mean nothing when they hurt our feelings, or do not quite meet our demands.

So, how do we learn to grow in a world of dysfunctions? How do we come to be whom we are to be, when in fact, we have grown from a difficult place? How does that happen? What is born inside of us that propels us, to where we need to be? Who can say . . . is it a driving strength? Is it deliberateness, a power that exceeds humanness? Is there an influence that we block and resist as part of anything that could or would possibly comprise the package that is manifest within us . . .? How does it happen? Why don't we know? Why?

Deep in my soul, somewhere so deep one cannot even imagine . . . somehow, someplace, so way down . . . I know! I know we are just one. Just simply one. One human creating itself a million, trillion ways. **That is GOD**... That's it. That's all of it. That is all it has ever been. I am you . . . you are me. When we really get it, the shift will begin. We will have come full circle and the knowledge of our divinity will reveal itself. *And* in a peaceful moment, we will know that which we truly are, far exceeds our grandest expectations of anything our earth life can ever explain.

In one heart*
Donna

People that I loved, friends that I adored and family that I held close to my heart, all but disappeared as I made my way through a new world **alone** . . . A shiver in my throat and tears on my soul, allowed me only to move with each waking moment. A mechanical motion, a living robot, is truly what I had become. I prayed for my sleep time, although difficult to succumb, it did help to reduce the number of hours I spent trying to function.

I questioned my mind. How did this happen? How could this be? As James Ray famous author and thriving entrepreneur with a background in behavioral sciences puts it, in one of his most recent videos . . . *"In our greater universe if you're not growing then you are dying."* Well I felt almost dead and for sure I knew a higher, bigger thing had all but snipped my branches and to make any sense of it . . . was just impossible.

I guess that's how it is; I discovered the ability and the words to produce this series. When you have lived it; it is not difficult to convey. So if by chance you think I do not know what you are going through or where you have been, trust me, you are so wrong. I think also, that's another complexity we as average humans all seem to suggest, we see someone in the media and they have become successful and we think "yeh right, they haven't been through this!" Well, I know now that is also not true because, if you are reading my book, then . . . **I am a living example.**

From my heart to yours, please understand you are no different than me. Propelled by a power greater than you are . . . and with the help of an effort on your part, which is already provided within your soul, you will **stand up** . . . and once again, find **your success!**

So are they right or are they wrong? Am I right, or am I wrong? We are no doubt, talking about the people the friends and the family around you, that are pointing a finger or through your situation you have lost, along the way. Let's also be clear. You are in the middle of your crisis and not everybody is doing and saying what you think you need to hear or feel, right at this time.

You know you are in a weakened state . . . *"what the heck is wrong with them, why can't they be a little easier on me, after all they know I am suffering,"* you are thinking and even more so, questioning yourself. Hello! This is so important. **This is judgment** when we come into **enlightenment** and this is critical to our healing . . . **there is no judgment**.

Now don't expect people or things to be different because you feel you have come into clarification, because make no mistake, they won't be! You just won't expect them to be and you will handle your reaction very differently. This is a difficult step in your journey and how long it will take you, or how many knocks and blows you will need to get it . . . is simply up to you.

Without question or concern you are picking it apart, first of all there is no right or wrong. In the everyday scheme of things it is what it is. Remember the words I set before you . . . **"It is a changing thing"** and when we change **we are taking steps toward growth.** Now, how many steps do we need to take? Well, I am still taking knocks and blows and I am many years into my changing thing, life goes on . . .

Remember again, this is your lesson and as I have stated before, there are countless symptoms and pretty much, the stages we must experience to arrive at a better destination are in fact . . . most commonly the same. We just have different situations and circumstances.

So reviewing today's format realize, when you question . . . you are in a state of examination, **yes examination.** Your preoccupation with your situation is exactly what you need to be doing. Please understand this happens most times, in the early stages of your crisis, however, continues for a very long time. This step can more appropriately be referred to as **self examination.**

In life we struggle. Oh gosh, we struggle through the day by day. We are caught up in what is going on, never realizing there is a bigger, larger us behind the experience that needs to surface. That bigger, greater thing that we really are, wants to bear its tender emotion. That which is actually our soul, is right there in the middle of life's chaos.

Ok so we have a situation. We work with someone in a position of authority that demonstrates low average behavior. She does not lead by example, shrugs her duties and shows little concern for her team, creating resentment and angry temper among the group.

Now our first reaction is to tell her off and most of us do. However, when we come into our own amazing wisdom, we learn to talk to our soul before we talk to anyone else. A silent contemplation with GOD and most quickly we discover a way to handle this with peace and grace.

So many times it is more than difficult as most people are not on the same page, peace is the last thought in their world. Even trying to address the situation gently, can often cause a rise and an extreme flare up can easily come out of a few quick and simple words.

Does it mean that we should stop trying? Should we give up on that wrong doer? Sometimes we are not aware that our job is already done. Most times we think like average humans. We are just working together. We don't have to know, care about, or try to help this other person. When in truth your time shared was actually destiny and you were brought to that place, to that moment to render a service . . . *and not by chance!*

You for sure are giving or getting something your soul is readily seeking out. Many times though, it is so incidental that our humanness does not even catch it. It could be a simple spoken word, or a specific characteristic that someone needed to witness. Yes, in all circumstance you are the giver or the taker. *And for sure a power far greater than yourself recognizes this. And so . . . I offer a simple suggestion . . . "give yourself a hug and let it go."*

🦋 I am in my garage this morning going through bins filled with my books, so many they could build a mountain created from paper alone. It is no wonder a power has allowed this material to come through me. I am working on my portfolio for this very purpose... My former life would bring me to this place in time, rummaging through old papers and the like.

I need to recreate the memory of who I was, so I could once again acclaim the recognition of a woman, with a desperate passion to be the lady restaurant owner; a dream that began in my mind as a small child. This was my reality in earlier days.

With a painstaking perseverance I created a world for myself in **DiMarco's Restaurant,** A tiny place off the beaten path . . . that grew with the magnitude of a giant, for a neighborhood spot.

I make a point here . . . this is how we become who we really are. Nothing comes easy. It is with laborious effort that the gift of greatness is born. The creation of a fine artist, the profound words of a unique author and the matrix of a higher intelligence that thrives within us, comes to the forefront. Miraculously, it produces your passion **through you**, as if you would have constructed this monumental design all by your self. Was it a book, was it a painting, did you build a sky scraper? Well, these things do happen every day.

So when we have a burning desire to do a thing, **GOD** and the universe and all the powers that may . . . go to work just for you! However, that happens both ways. If your design is for a higher purpose, then greatness is born. Now, if your design is to cheat, lie or steal simply stated, to do a bad thing . . . then like the other, so too is your misfortune created and suddenly, that monumental purpose seems quite minuscule . . . compared to the agony you must endure.

This is how **we grow** and this is how **we learn.** Know it or not... you are the **miracle** that is **creating it all.**

In pursuit of our journey the road we travel in life, most often, is quite difficult to endure. Knowledge of this prompts me to understand how it is; my soul has the gracious ability to have been allowed, to greet the arrival of this moment. I consider this thought in stillness and it triggers my peacefulness with **GOD.**

This is the hunt in our human physicality, in a vast universe filled with uncertainty, that **we find peace**. How and when that miracle happens is quite another story. Now, this is the real glitch . . . only our perception of it allows us, to create that which we seek. Surely peace is a gift.

So then to be certain . . . how do we make sure we are to bring the gift to ourselves and not the gauge? Just in the pondering of the thought, we call a fear upon us! Absolutely, this is an addiction among so many people today.

You have a situation; weather it be good or bad is quite irrelevant. It could very well be the beginning of something you might like to see yourself accomplish. This does not mean our example need show you trying to set a world record, or become a movie star. Your situation could be even minuscule, something as small as buying a pair of jeans or what you will serve at your next dinner party.

At the onset, first thought is in line with your need to do a thing and so too, is the power within you, there to meet your need to accomplish exactly what you set out after. So, how is it that so many times we think we are steadfast and on the right track . . . ? Things just do not go our way.

Well, allow me to leave you with this uncomplicated thought. Do you think when you set out to purchase those jeans, your concern over that extra ten pounds you have gained most recently . . . and also knowing you really could not afford to buy them to begin with . . . had anything to do with that rude woman that grabbed those jeans right off that rack? Even while you stood there and watched you were not able to catch them quickly enough, in spite of how badly you wanted them. And then . . . to have words with her right in the middle of the store.

🦋 In the wisdom of our years we come to realize that we really never had anything to do with this at all. That at every turn, each time we tried to conduct the progression of our lives; every single approach to make a plan . . . occurred exactly the opposite of what we had designed, in fact, each scenario, a mystery and many times, a shocking event to say the least.

Suddenly it becomes crystal clear, it is almost frightening. How could this be? What controls all of this? Who and what really is controlling me? Why can't we know? Why?

Why the big secret? No less, in the center of the illusion we experience in this human condition, we cannot deny free will. It is there. Free will and choice so to speak, begin immediately. Yes, instant life!

A human angel has just left the birth canal and somehow the tiny infant feels its first cramp, its very first air bubble . . . and choice takes its first step. A decision must be made . . . cramp?

Yes or no? Cramp . . . cry or sleep? You are not even here sixty seconds and yes, life happens and you are thrown right into it! A journey begins, it is your ride and every step of the way you are making choices, or at least you are reared to believe so.

Years begin to fly by. You are just trying to get through each situation and suddenly you realize each scenario is getting tougher and tougher. That gut wrenching feeling, the one that seems like it is scratching your soul, begins to eat at you! What the hell is going on here, you begin to question.

The guy you love is leaving you, you gave him your heart, and you say to yourself . . . I didn't pick this. You're struggling; no matter how hard you try . . . you can't seem to make enough money, then suddenly you fall and collect thousands of dollars and sure that's a help. Yet you are left with an injury and live in pain every day. You say again to yourself . . . I didn't pick this. More and more upheaval takes hold of your existence. A child is born, a parent dies, a home is built, a job is lost. One moment you are filled with joy and the next, tears wet your life like raindrops. Sure you question, you bet you do.

And then somehow, suddenly as you approach the finish line of your life, an awareness takes hold of you, it's almost as if a door opens in your mind and you get to take a peek *And in a silent moment* you know, ***you just know*** it is **GOD**. A something bigger, a thing you cannot see or touch, hear or feel, yet some magical way . . . **you just know it is GOD**. It always has been and it has **propelled your every move!**

🕊 It is always a lesson; there is no getting around it. If you take a closer look, if you really, really stand back and watch your life just day by day whatever it is, then without question you must know a grander intelligence has chartered your course.

It is like taking a ride. You have learned how to get to where you need to go, you just know the way and so if you accidentally took a wrong turn, of course, you would catch it. Maybe you were day dreaming or perhaps on the phone while you were driving or walking. That's it . . . that is how it happens, how we finally come to recognize that power, that magnificence, the thing we know deep within, so deep . . . we cannot even deny it to our own intelligence. **Again, that I call GOD.**

I am not having a good evening. I am sort of weepy, just disgusted with it all. Everyday I am reminded in my heart that my job is like living in a nightmare, I wish I could find something better. I am uncertain if I should even continue in this type of industry, if sales is really for me, yet I wonder if I were in a store that was run fairly, might I just love what I am doing, at odds about it all . . . I do nothing.

Having had not quite an argument, but uncomfortable words with my partner, this particular night . . . in my weepy and disgusted state of mind, I decide to walk in the mall and wonder into the same type of retail store I work in. Well, as luck would have it in a moments notice, I bond with the sales lady at the counter and she quickly calls the manager over and the next thing I know, I am interviewing for another position. I am readily told, not all stores are run so unfairly, and before I leave the business to please work with them . . . and I do. My retail journey continued, when I thought I was done.

Is this an accident? Did I walk in there for no reason, was it by chance or was I steered? I was caught up in an argument, not even dressed appropriately to apply for a job, and that was the last thing on my mind in the middle of a couples quarrel. Yet, here I am excited and ready to start a new position in an industry I do enjoy and really did not want to give up on yet. I think the older we get, the closer we come to our own amazing wisdom, that incredible power that allows us to clearly see we are a part of a system that knows exactly where we need to be, at any moment, in any circumstance, that same system . . . that magnificent intelligence that takes a seed and turns it into a tree, walked me right into that store! **This is GOD, only GOD,** it always has been and always will be, it just takes us a lifetime of knocks and blows to figure it out, or . . . we might not pay attention at all.

So, in simple truth, and in uncolored experience, just plain commonality, day by day . . . life goes on. And so too in the dimly lit existence of the average person, that must all but try to survive in our society as it really is . . . there is one question that looms upon us all, and always has and all-ways will.

One simple, yet furthermost supreme question remains in the minds of so many people today. One query goes unanswered. Undoubtedly, we all just land here, without the answer and for sure, nobody gets to stay forever. Ready or not, when your number is called, you're out of here! We really, really just don't know how it all happens.

Simple yet spellbinding, we arrive here not knowing where we come from and we leave here not knowing where we are going! Yet the vast majority will be the first to deny that a greater intelligence is in fact, orchestrating our every move. As I write these words for you this morning, most all of you, will be steadfast as you proclaim you are making all your own choices.

Nonetheless, the powerful question goes unanswered. We enter a world, this physicality with a search for evidence. We are riddled with uncertainty throughout the entire lifespan of our existence, all the while the unrequited obvious . . . lies within us!

Now, I can change the way I have presented this feature to you this morning. I can; in fact, write it with less passion, however, no one can deny what I have said here . . . is true.

So why do we try to **control everything**? Why do we try so hard, when things are going wrong? Should there not be that piece of us, even a tiny part . . . which understands the **mystery**?

Yes, there is a **magic within us** and yes, we can touch it . . . **with our minds.**

🦋 You have heard me say, sometimes your crisis happens at your own hand and sometimes your crisis happens at the hand of another and then, of course, there is the hand of GOD, that's the hand we will talk about this morning.

Let's take the man who goes along somewhat oblivious. He just moves through life quietly; accepts it all, pretty much as it comes along. Never bucks, never barks. Yes, he is the background guy. Nice guy, but nobody really bothers much with him. He is pretty quiet, actually he borders on boring. He is the guy you meet at the water cooler, you know, a quick nod and you're on your way. So, let's focus on him for just a moment if you will.

He is Joe typical, not flamboyant, not frivolous, just a simple quiet commoner. He has a nice little home, a couple of kids and a sweet wife. He never gives her much of a hard time . . . even when he knows, deep down he should! Rents a cabin once a year, takes the wife and kids to Michigan. He simply chooses a more passive path. Actually, he is **walking through life asleep**.

Then suddenly one Sunday morning he is in the bathroom mirror, brushing his teeth and hears a thud, steps into the kitchen to see what has fallen . . . and finds his wife dead on the floor! She is 42 years old and never has been sick a day in her life. Ok, you are going to say "Donna we don't like this example" neither do I, however, it speaks a powerful truth.

In a quick flash his life is upside down, what a horror, what heartache. Yet now the new guy must emerge . . . The change is upon him . . . like it or not. Now he must buck, he must bark. He has kids to raise, a house to pay for, a job to go to, when his heart is broken . . . and he wants to go to bed and cover his head . . . and die! **Now he is awake.**

This is GOD'S hand. Oh Lord . . . why? We question why? And I know your first response will be "well, what about her, why should she die so he could learn?" The answers will prevail in the weeks ahead.

Of life and death there is a season. Why it happens the way it does? Well many times it is conjured with little sense or even reason.

The query goes on and on. Understand we fly with the birds and swim with the fish, build buildings that touch the sky, and even drill holes to the center of our earth. Today exchanging body parts is almost like picking your favorite lipstick at the cosmetic counter. We go on line and if it takes more than six seconds we are impatient of the wait.

And the debate of miracles is all but negated at every turn. In our world just breathing is a miracle and yet we do not grasp the capacity of our provisions.

The face of synchronicity plays a measure of mystery within the entire span of our earth function and humanness and we don't question it, nor even realize the grander vision. There are no mistakes, you arrive here with a roadmap and you are going to follow it no matter what.

My busgirl gets killed on her way home from work. There is dirt on the side of the road, that sends her car reeling and brings her life to a crashing halt! She could not brake quickly enough, yet so many vehicles were unable to brake quickly enough in that very same exact spot. They are fine. "Just another scary moment" the driver concludes, as he catches his breath from the fright of his skid and proceeds home safe and sound. Think about it. Think hard.

It is a preplanned field trip and you are here for the excursion. You will make all the right moves, in spite of your will or want to participate in much of the upheaval. *And* for sure, every step of the way you will think it is your idea, your choice.

Trust me, it's planned and **GOD** has packed your bags and **GOD** alone will set those bags where he chooses. It is that simple. **We fight...** but when we give up the struggle **we find peace in the journey.**

🦋 "When things go wrong as they sometimes will . . ." It seems we've all heard that line before and yes, the words carry a powerful meaning. For sure you can count on things going wrong and they do and they will. Can an awareness of this analogy of our agenda we call life then help to soften the knocks and blows? Well, I do not know that anything out there can really ever powder puff your catastrophe.

In simple terms, when tragedy reaches our doorstep it is like no other. Neither nor any one's horror can be as difficult to bear as our own. Why? Why is ours always the worse? What makes this so? Well, unquestionably because we own it. It is ours.

The guy next door can have three heart surgeries and be told things aren't looking good if a fourth is needed and we might want to suggest he buck up at the first groan of despair. On the other hand, we can take a fall and need four stitches, which would pale in comparison and yet, still think we have a right to wail for the next three months and many times do.

So, again we question what allows us to be the way we are? How many times do you wish you might have shut your mouth, but you didn't? How many times do you think you acted too quickly, but could not slow the movement that only created a situation that brought you more tears and more heartache? Why? Why do we behave the way we do and should we try harder to practice more control?

Well, I liken it to a knee jerk reaction. Sometimes life deals us a swift blow and we retaliate in the same quick unthinkable fashion and then go back and question our hurried behavior. We should not! We should not question our previous actions. We should not question at all. Ok, so how? Is there an easier way? Is there, in fact, a better way at all?

Oh yes, there is . . . and only when we step into the awareness of **"Divine Order"** and the power it creates within us to move through any situation, *do we touch the peacefulness of GOD.*

"Day by day in every way I am getting better and better."

Emil Coue'

And so it is time in our moment of self examination, that we must look at the "how and why" of our daily trivialities. What must it take for us to step back and glance, yes quite simply view our behavior, recognize our reactions and choose peace in our lives?

Susan Jeffers eloquently states her claim in "Embracing Uncertainty" her life affirming audio book, I felt played a dramatic role in helping me find peace in my time of urgency and despair.

What is the magic we must find that takes us from the worry and brings us to the wonder of it all? How does this simple transition become a daily ritual in the parameters of our existence?

I believe when you attach yourself to **Divine Order**, you learn to trust an intelligence, a source energy, you cannot see. **In doing so faith is born!** That supply is always alive and available within you and ready to serve your needs. Faith alone is the one single greatest tool in our reality and always has been, and yes . . . always will be. In a world tainted with dysfunction, today we recognize the need more than ever. In faith, not religion . . . in Faith, peace is the reward.

And so I do not want you to feel that I am against religion. Surely, that would not be true. You need to know what works for you. You may or may not follow a creed. That is your call. Just allow me to be clear, in religion someone is telling you what to believe in . . . in faith you believe in yourself. That power, **the power of GOD** is in you. It is simply nestled within your mind . . . **And with that power you can light up the world!**

It has been said and only in truth, it is like a movie picture show and you are the star. Yes, now you can watch "the *not so good things you do"* just know . . . each lesson gives us an opportunity to redo our bad things . . . *"And make them very good."*

So many times we do not even recognize the losses in our lives until the conflict is actually already over. Then one day your old and the birth of an amazing wisdom you understand, you really never had at all in former days, somehow has miraculously, set in. You can almost feel it, *"this wisdom"* it is there in your bones, it is in your heart, it is your most precious soul, coming alive . . . winning. Yes, winning . . . over your ego!

Your old, however, you have come to love yourself. With a complete and determined and even, unquestionable absoluteness . . . you finally love who you are.

Then as if someone washed the window in your mind, there is a clarity in your awareness you have never known. You begin to pile the different catastrophic occurrences in your life and suddenly you know, somehow, it is clear and yes, you just know . . . what has been missing all along.

In this example it has been a man issue, one loss, one poor relationship after another. Yet, you never paid attention to the fact that your daddy died when you were three. You just accepted you were fatherless . . . you just didn't get one. He was taken away, taken by GOD . . . so GOD must be right, you just didn't deserve one and you live through all of your heartaches, never really realizing you needed a dad all along.

These situations happen in a thousand different ways; each occurrence specific to the human that must bear the discomfort, and we just don't get it, till and only that amazing wisdom, the clarity . . . I refer to as that unseen thing, that intelligent magic, that knows exactly what you need, and perpetually understands what is required of you to arrive at that perfect destination, I call your journey! Yes, the one you travel over a span of a lifetime.

That incomparable, most overwhelming phenomena, that genius, that brings you precisely what you need, when you need it . . . **I call GOD.**

So is there a better time for us to have gained the knowledge that grows with us through our struggles? Perhaps if so, our experiences might just be different and our lessons not well learned. How clever **"the Master that holds the key"** to your perfect portal and the wit to know, just when to let you in . . . on it all.

"I do not ask for any crown
But that which all may win;
Nor try to conquer any world
Except the one within."

                              Louisa May Alcott

I sat starring and the words just came, I knew they were meant for all of you.

The tree outside my window is a beautiful site. It needs nothing to accomplish its task. It comes fully equipped. In all its natural splendor it contains all of the amenities a universe might offer . . . the light of a sun to help it grow . . . the rain from a cloud to keep it cleansed . . . the air of a wind to allow it to breathe and the soil from a ground that can only permit it to grow more trees.

And it need only sit there in all of its loveliness . . . this is Magic! We all find mystery in magic; we are awed with the imagination it creates within us. We are moved with its power. We are stunned with the incredible, mystical wonder that magic alone can produce.

Yet, we look at a tree and know this is GOD and do not see the wonder . . . do not grasp the magic, are not stunned with the marvel of the power that has truly created us. Why? Why, do we not trust? Why do we not see? Why do we not trust GOD to walk us where we really need to be? Why? **The very same GOD that constructed a tree constructed a human, and that would be you and I.**

You come fully equipped. GOD has fueled its very power within you to accomplish your task here. That intelligence, that higher consciousness is right there . . . within you.

Yet, we cannot grasp the magic. We must fret and fumble. We choose to sigh not sing, when the song has already been written, just for you, written with your magic. Yet you do not see the wonder and then wonder, why you fall . . . *when in truth you are a tree, nothing less nor more . . . at all.*

"Feeling the icy kick, the endless waves
reaching around my life, I moved my arms
and coughed, and in the end saw land."

Mary Oliver

"The Swimming Lesson." I love her words; they played a significant roll in many tender moments I have experienced. I recited them into a friend's ear in the last hours of her life, as she waited to die. I also prayed them amongst a small group of bar people that frequented my establishment *"DiMarco's Restaurant"* for a fellow that sat at the corner of my bar, most days of the week. No, he was not a drunk, just lonely and needed conversation. I never thought I would come to know that feeling. He died with no family or friends and we put together a small prayer hour for him. I did not know his faith and used her poem, the message was powerful and he was so worthy of the small effort we made.

Her poetry is available in most libraries and book stores and so worth the read; it brings to mind the endless struggle that life's journey presents to us every day.

In the water we are drowning, groping and grasping for that tiniest molecule of air, the substance we cannot see or touch or feel, nonetheless, must have . . . must get it somehow, somewhere, just to breathe. Feeling the weight of the water pulling us down, deeper and deeper, we must fight to find that tiny bubble to fill our lungs and we do! On land, we flounder like a fish out of the water and the fight continues.

The fight for life. We fight for our freedom. We fight for our rights. We fight for our families, our friends, our jobs, we fight for what we have and we fight, for what we don't have! We are taught to fight. Well, there is another small cliché and really, I do not know where I ever heard these words or who said this, but that it makes perfect sense, *"If you are meant to be shot . . . you will never drown."* So the query, once again comes to the forefront . . . Why do we fight?

Why do we fight when we know there is a thing we need, we cannot see or touch. Why don't we understand the simple greatness of what we are? Why can't we trust the uncomplicated intelligence that we know, cannot be seen, or even felt . . . when we don't even know how we got here or where we will go. **Why don't we know that this is GOD?** Why can't we see that this road is already paved. Why can't we give up the fight and step into the power of peace . . . we so deserve?"

When a heart is broken, the tears that weep cleanse our soul. We wonder why, why did this have to happen? Why did I have to meet him, after all, I was just feeling so healed from the last broken relationship? Why again . . . why GOD? Why again?

Well, is there a grander reason? Are we not sick of reasons anyway? Is that angry disgust for the entire situation not part of a continuance to create the ongoing lesson from ever ending? Can we ever really be sure about any of this?

My sister meets a guy at sixteen years old, stays with him, marries him and spends her entire lifetime with only this man. I on the other hand have gone through a mountain of men. What does it mean? Is one better than the other? Am I just destined for more people and more lessons? Who created this? Me? Her? Is there some mysterious relationship handbook, I never received upon entering my life on earth? Was it supposed to be read to me, while I was in the womb preparing to make my great entrance?

How can we know? How can we really ever know? Life in of itself is magical! If only we could breathe and just suck in every moment filled with joy, simply have everything we ever want. No sadness . . . No suffering . . . No struggle.

Now let's just think about that statement. Well, I have. Of course, I am a mover and a shaker, but . . . what would we really do? C'mon seriously, what would we really do? Would it be fun to just lie around and do absolutely nothing, because life was so perfect?

Were Adam and Eve on a mission to destroy there paradise on purpose? Could they have been bored with their little perfect nest? I am guessing yes! Yes, of course, yes . . . *And* they set the trend. They said, "let's mix it up and let's have some fun, let's make life interesting." "Let's have to figure it all out on our own as we go along, thanks GOD for doing a great job, but we have to take over now." "Take control . . . do our own thing."

And so, I couple humor with homage for the two beginners, however, please understand *the vast majority of humans still do not realize, they **just don't trust the intelligence that is always there to guide them through all of their hurdles! And so . . . as a result, so many times, you trip and fall and that very power, the power I reference as GOD, picks you up and yet . . . you still do not recognize the call.*** 🕊

In my heart spot there is GOD I struggle through life's toughest moments, yet know somehow, some magical way, it will be better. What is this? What gives us an ability to come through a nightmare and still immerge as a star? Literally, a luminary compared to where we have been and the mud we have experienced in our catastrophe. This for sure, is where miracles are born and we don't even notice the blessing in it all.

How do we come up with the courage? Where does that courage really come from? Who and what supplies it? Well the courage itself is in fact, **the miracle.** We know we cannot walk into a store and purchase the product. Truly if we could bottle it and sell it, would that not be great.

Well, we don't have to pay. Courage is free. Courage is an instinct that cannot be bought, no different than your spirit, your psyche and your soul. It is a certain something an availability already there, there within you. Yes, like all else, ready for you to grasp its very essence . . . and all you need to do . . . to get it . . . **Is suffer!**

I know it's a scary thought; yet again, I must reinforce the very words I have repeated with grace . . . and to remind you it comes with an amazing wisdom . . . If you are paying attention and if you have taken even some of what I have offered you in these weeks of reflection through this writing, then you have started a connection with the quiet understanding, that smack in the middle of your crisis, you are still **learning** and you are still **growing.**

Please also know that until you comprehend the full capacity of why your incident has happened, you will continue to experience more lessons and they will . . . very likely include more **suffering**

🕊 It is what it is. You are caught right smack in the middle of your calamity and for the life of you, you cannot understand how something so horrid could even possibly be happening to you. I do not care what it is, it does not matter. You can count on it, it is usually a blow! I am definitely going to say some things now that are critical to your comprehending the full capacity of what I am trying to convey.

Are you divorcing a man you love madly, or possibly, he is leaving you? Either way, it just does not matter. A change is set in motion. Different people will start to come into your life, yes different people. Different situations and different heart aches that you have begun to experience, start a process of transition, some yours, some belonging to the person you have come to know, perhaps you work with, or somehow met because of your split. There could be all manner of experiences occurring just because of your divorce.

Your separation which is undoubtedly heartache has created new people, new places and new things. It is a roadmap, a journey we don't notice or even recognize. Iyanla Vansant states it most clearly in her book "Faith in the Valley" and I may have mentioned it prior in earlier writings, but that's ok . . . it bears repeating. This is like school and rest is your diploma and when you finally get it and by the time we do, we are generally pretty old, and you are out of here. Rest is your reward, in earth terms we call it death.

So, maybe you locked the door on your successful business, like I did. Maybe you lost your home, or maybe you are stricken with a horrible disease. Again, it does not matter, in any and all adversity you are forced next to that new person and new situations are happening with you and around you. **Why? Well simply because** you are here to serve. **Yes, you are here to serve that person next to you** . . . or even more so, they may very well be **serving you**, it works both ways, however, that is clearly the only reason we are really here. We are here to experience and to serve.

It might only be a few words someone needs to hear, or you could be the someone needing to listen. It could possibly be a two year dialogue or a whole new life with a whole new person or persons that will teach you, what you need to know. Places and things that require only your ability to help and it is disguised as your crisis, calamity and or heartache... again, call it what you like. You are serving and it is **GOD'S work getting done!** Now, make no mistake **only GOD and your higher power puts that plan together for you.** Remember the puzzle pieces . . . from earlier messages.

Nothing real can be threatened.
Nothing unreal exists.
Herein lies the peace of God.

A Course in Miracles

There is no question, we have a world true only to dysfunction. This insanity is everywhere. People killing people, planes blowing up buildings, children shooting other children, bones found everyday that have been cut up and dismembered with no regard for the life that has been dragged through terror!

For sure it all hinges on an ego . . . an ego that is thirsty for evil . . . an ego that is hungry, angry, lonely and tired, an ego that lives in jealousy and greed. So the question remains. Without this ego would there not be perfection?

Ordinary people, ordinary places and ordinary things, are all of an exterior component that our most honored books, will teach you do not exist . . . but they do . . . well in our human scope, they do. In ordinary circumstance the ego exists and for sure without it, there would be no teaching, on this premise alone, how would we learn? Without teaching and learning there can be no circumstance, no existence . . . yes again, without these very elements it would mean to negate the process . . . the process of this physicality, this moment, this one instant of life, we experience in this one miniscule of light . . . the light that has created us. Magic, this is our magic, the intelligence we cannot see or feel or touch, that places us in this space . . . this slot in time!

One might say "how dare you" without these things you mention. Why imply negation to the process, would it not . . . or . . . could it not mean perfection? Yes, yes with an astounding consciousness the answer is yes! It would only mean perfection and in perfection there can only be love. When you have love there is only joy and peace and in peace there is only **GOD**. In our earth time our presence in this space; we are placed here simply to learn this. In our arena the negation is perfection and in our struggle, our crisis, our calamity, this most horrific thing happening to us . . . we are taught the truth and when we come into truth . . . **we come into GOD.**

When we come into **GOD**, we are contained in this one instant in time, this one miniscule flash of energy and light, that ultimately spans a **lifetime. Yes, this is our life**, squeezed into this one moment . . . and through this negation, it can only be . . . **our perfection.**

🦋 I am one with GOD. Through GOD I can do anything. No task too large nor too small. No heartache to great I cannot bear, no tear I cannot shed, no darkness I cannot turn to light. There would be no voice, I cannot hear or understand . . . no miracle I cannot create, not even a devastation I cannot overcome. To this promise, I hold true. I am one with GOD, I am it all! I am held tenderly, gingerly in the sweet hands of an intelligence, a magic, I cannot express in human terms.

Tragedy strikes and average day to day reaction cannot carry us through. This trauma calls for a special conduct, but how, how can one display an out of the ordinary protocol when a heart is broken, or a loss is so great that even to breathe . . . is a task.

Yet these occurrences are on our plate more than not and the average human can all but crumble beneath rubble far too heavy to bear. What can we do? Where can we turn? When it is so bad that even to speak is more than a heart can allow, what can we do? There is nothing left. No talking, no thinking, no tear, not angel nor demon can relieve a soul in so much pain, so much strife, the burden so big . . .we pray to die.

And so in a most critical moment, a moment of helplessness, a most tender moment of hopelessness, we can only turn inward and go to the very deepest, most internal part of who we really are and in so doing, we call upon a thing we think, is really not even there. Yet know somehow, some crazy way . . . it is the only account that will actually help. I call this **numinous source,** this magical essence within our skin . . . **GOD**! In your final moment of sorrow . . . you must willfully know, this is all there is and all there ever has been and all there ever will be . . . **and it is readily available to lift you up.**

In the caverns of our minds, therein lies the power of GOD. Here is where your true journey begins . . . here is where your path unfolds. It is within you that your existence is born. As surely as you are one with GOD so too are you the miracle created and the paradox deep within your soul, can and will only allow you to know you are also the creator.

So, how can we touch this place? How can we know we are GOD, created by the power, one with the power, one in the same . . . to do "all that he has done and even greater things?"

It is only in silence that a power greater than yourself reveals the magic, the miracle that you truly are. It is only in your quiet place that mind, spirit and reality, all come together. This is where you can know the incredible mystery of an intelligence you cannot see; this is where you touch **GOD**! It is in silence that spirit claims a measure of movement and as surely as the raindrop turns into a snowflake and the heat of a sun melts it down to magically allow it to disappear, so too does that same spirit move within you and is one with you . . . and is you!

Is it by chance you flick a switch and light fills the room? Someone created that, someone had the thought and brought it into existence... we all know the tale of the light bulb. We all know the story of Thomas Edison and his burning desire to create electricity. Well, he was the very same human being you are. What made him so special? What intelligence allowed him the gift and why? Why him and not you?

I pray to a higher consciousness to supply the answers, so that I may provide them for all of you . . . **and I know that decision will only prevail . . . through the hand of God.**

"Surrender is faith that the power of love can accomplish anything even when you cannot foresee the outcome."

Deepak Chopra

The power of love . . . Love. The very power of love. I admire these words, they resemble the sentiment of my own mind and heart, and in simple agreement of them, I am in thought of the actual perception they present.

The presence of a butterfly when it swoops down near you in magnificent color, that moves you to wonder.

The birth of a life form . . . a baby, an animal, a fish . . . any and all, a product of which we know not yet, in truth, where we really begin.

The powerful force of a moving ocean that leaves you breathless in its attendance and touches your core.

The sky in the early hours as darkness leaves and the morning light begins to illuminate the clouds that float above our world, with no ropes to neither hold nor bind them. You are awed!

The silence of a moment when your heart beats in fear and your call is to GOD.

I can go on and on, all that I mention here are truly moments of love . . . simple and powerful, the essence of which takes us off our feet. Yet, somehow none compare . . . to the soft whisper of a lover's breath that caresses your ear as he lay near you in restful moments. When you need his hand, his hand is there . . . There to hold you, there to carry you when you cannot stand on your own. There to laugh with you, cry with you, dream with you, there to be your best friend and your greatest support . . . this is love.

A sea, a sky, a tear of a baby cry . . . in all of these there is woman, then man, the productivity of an intelligence that cannot, or ever will be . . . defined in human terms.

I dedicate this inscription to my dearest friend Cora and her new husband Larry, married June 27th in the year of 2009.

"Any idiot can face a crisis,
it's the day to day living that wears you out."

Jo Ryan

As part of our human condition there are more than a few obstacles we will endure a long the way, and also as part of that very same agenda, will be our reaction to them.

If something or somebody frightens us we are going to feel fear. If something or somebody angers us we are going to feel angry, going along with that same thought process, if something or somebody extends their kindness, goes out of their way to make us happy, we will feel joy.

Our first response, the initial reaction to life's knocks and blows is simply that part which is not changeable; the snow leaves and spring has sprung and a tiny seedling burst through the soil and produces a flower . . . that will never change! You open your eyes to the morning sunlight and close them to evening darkness . . . that will never change, birds fly and fish swim and that will never change.

Your reaction to what happens to you . . . that first initial response . . . will never change. If somebody scares you, you are supposed to be scared. Your time to think and what you will do with that does not occur till after "initial response." We so often blame our selves for our reactions when that is simply part of our *human condition*, that part which is not changeable.

Does it help to know these things? I think it depends on the extent of your situation and your tolerance for life.

The crux of our message today though, is that we are human . . . **give yourself a hug and move on!**

Surrender . . . **Surrender**; when you surrender to a thing, it is amazing what happens. And don't we hate it. Really, think about it. We hate to give in and most times and for the vast majority of our society, we cannot bear to give up. We see it in our personal lives, we see it in our wars and we witness it . . . in our government everyday.

You are caught up in the middle of your crisis, your calamity. You are flat out broke. You have lost a solid position. It does not matter what it was. Was it a business, was it a job, a contract, who cares . . . it really just does not matter. It is behind you now and the toughest thing you have to do . . . is step forward and most times your pocket is empty.

One simple single step will change your life . . . but how? How does it happen, when you are lost you cannot find your way, you are trying, GOD only knows, with your whole heart . . . yet, everything you try just doesn't seem to fit. You are frustrated and you just don't understand and for sure and without question, you know you are not one to give up. So you ask yourself "what the hell am I suppose to do now?"

Oh well, all your good friends will tell you to just "hang in there." *And* that is exactly how you're feeling right about now . . . like you are "hanging there" somewhere, just lost in time or space and any second, that rope is gonna give out and you are going to fall . . . You are scared to death!

It is generally right about this time you realize, you have tried everything. There is just nothing else you know how to do, in this particular moment, you are exasperated, done in and done out and all you really can do . . . is just . . . give up! It is scary, GOD knows, I know . . . but generally, right at this point **surrender steps in.** Yes, it takes all of this and **surrender** finally takes over and now, this is when **you turn to your power that special place** . . . I remind you, once again . . . you cannot see or touch or even feel and a **magical peace** comes over you and you are finally able to say to yourself, "Ok whatever happens, happens" *And* that very power . . . ***that power I call GOD responds to your core*** and you just know somehow, the next step is going to happen exactly the way it is suppose to . . . in spite of yourself.

And so the power is in us to do great things and somehow I just do. In a moments notice life changes all on its own. You see we think we are doing it, we think we are creating our world; building our successes and living our failures . . . when, in fact, it is an unseen thing that is doing it all. Where is it? Well, who in the hell knows. think about it, who in the hell really knows anything . . . about this arena, whatsoever! Or do we?

The one thing I do know for sure is accepting what we cannot change is a monumental step in the face of healing. It does not happen easy and it doesn't even happen until you finally just give up. That is what everybody calls **"letting go."** It is not really you learning to be cool about your calamity; it is just you, at the end of your rope.

You finally give up and don't give a hell about where and how you fall! You feel like your jumping through hoops, and you are . . . yet, you also realize you are getting through it. Now, what it is does not matter . . . (Repeating myself) it could be a job loss, it could be an illness, or even a death. It could even be . . .all of the above. You just want it done and finally the toughest part is.

Suddenly, oh so suddenly . . . the miracle immerges, forces its way through . . . and as if you step into another zone, another place in time . . . *you are at peace.* That without question or doubt *I call GOD.* That, for sure, is the unseen thing, the incredible intelligence, you cannot touch, but somehow, some incremental way, you know is working for you.

And so, in the middle of your strife you stand a little taller, you feel a little lighter. Yes, in small moments you definitely notice a change . . . something different . . . and without complete recognition of origin, you simply come into awareness. **You are the change** and somewhere deep down, so deep, a voice within speaks to you in silence and echoes "in the middle of this mess I have grown." "Today I am proud, so proud of who I am."

In my most difficult times I have been kind. I have understood the human next to me, the complicated being, bearing tender feelings they do not understand or even acknowledge. Without frenzy, I accept they are in their own space. I learn to listen and be still in my anxiety and go along with **GOD'S plan for me.** I just know now, we really do not have to suffer to grow. The invisible power of **GOD** just gives us the nudge, to be . . . **certain that we do.**

"Things don't change, we change."

Henry David Thoreau

🦋 Hope. What is hope? Well, there is always hope. Hope changes everything. When you're in hope, you are not giving up. So, really what is it? When you are in hope, you are alive, excited and waiting . . . you are just wishing and wondering. You are simply day dreaming into the future . . .

In hope there is more, there is also sometimes less. Something is in front of you or, something is behind you. Yes, that's it. You think it is finally behind you. You are through it now . . . now, the worst is over. Things have changed. We think it is a new day and things will always be better and then, all of a sudden . . . something goes wrong.

Once more, your chin is back on the floor! How could this be happening to me again? How could this be **GOD? HOW?** So, there we go . . . putting it back on GOD. Well, in the words of a most famous author, yes you read at the onset. "Things don't change." We are making all the changes.

We forget. We forget, that people are not going to treat us any better, just because we have grown. We have grown, yet most times, they have not and only still think their way is the way it should be. We forget that life is what it is . . . and it will continue to allow us to experience knocks and blows, because that is what life does and it won't stop and not especially, just because we might think . . . we have had too many.

And so it is a process, a constant process and we must learn, to choose peace over power. So please be sure, in doing so, we can only lean on that intelligence, again, we cannot touch or see, that supreme essence we know is **GOD.**

We learn clearly to understand that we are guided, steered in a direction that will serve only our higher ability and we can move with that in stillness . . . and be peaceful and joyful within ourselves, and again, this is the only way . . . we come to know **GOD!**

I dedicate this correspondence to my dearest friend Kathy...
January 7, 1952 / January 6, 2012

She never gave up **hope . . .** 🦋

Today I am soon to be alive 73 years. I woke out of bed having a light bulb moment. It is so hard getting old, yet so great to have aged. In aging we come into amazing wisdom. Our very own amazement, through life experience.

Think of it, this journey from the time we first open our tiny infant eyes till now . . . one blow after the other. All the grief, heartache and sadness we leave behind us each day. How many people have disappointed us along the way, we cannot even say.

Each experience, as tough as they may be when the difficulty presents itself, teaches us one more . . . better way to be. In every hurtful occurrence, each grief stricken moment, whatever it is, however it happens . . . a child, a job, a house, a car, a love story, an illness, who knows . . . what matter, we come away most times, holding something against somebody!

The endless, senseless grudge . . . we have learned to create and then live each day while it tares on our heart and eats at our soul, sets the stage for us to learn. *And we do!*

So today I open my eyes, the same peepers that started this journey all those years ago, and I am at peace with myself and all things that encompass my world . . . and so, ah ha my light bulb moment, and I know that I am resolved . . . and so I question, how could this be. I know somehow it only happens one way, one magical way.

As my power, my GOD . . . that nameless intelligence we cannot quite get a hold of . . . has carried me through each calamity it taught me something very special, to find peace we must forgive and in that, we become who we really are!

And so I have forgiven and the list is endless... my mother, my father, my sister, my brother, my aunt, my uncle, the people I work with and the people that have worked for me, my lovers, my husbands and that lady trying to grab those shoes off the sale rack that I really want. I have forgiven everything and everybody and, in that . . . **I have found peace.** I wish that for all of you.

Ok so we are discussing forgiveness, what that really means and what that really does for us. Let's stay with this a moment longer and see what we come up with.

Well, when I say "forgive" that does not mean you have to be chum buddies with the person you feel has harmed you in some way. Now also understand someone does not have to beat your brains in to have hurt you. Many times words have a far greater effect on our emotions and anything physical can all but hardly compare.

When someone hurts our tender feelings not only is it a broken heart, but most times it is also a broken spirit, that part of us that is all but more difficult to try to put back together. You see our spirit is really who we are. The "who" part of us that touches that magnificence that moves us. That magic that fills our lungs with the air we breathe . . . that marvel that stimulates our legs so we can cover the track we tread. **This is GOD!**

You see we never give mind, or pay heed, to that unseen thing that has created our universe, our mystical, magical earth life that we so take for granted. The sky we look at, the ground we walk on, this vehicle we call our body, which functions with a precision that allows you to see and hear, to touch and taste, to take part of a miraculous journey that covers a life span. Your life, your most precious life!

SO here you are accepting that something or somebody can hurt your psyche, your tender feelings. No we will not own that. **No one gets to hurt us any longer when we discover we can detach.** Now how we separate ourselves is quite another story. Perhaps you are stuck with that person. Maybe it is a family member or someone that is part of a program that encompasses your world. How do we detach when all the while we are really attached?

We detach by knowing we are the bigger, better person. We detach by knowing that our bodies and minds have become a piece of steel, armor no words or hurtful innuendoes and or accusations can indeed penetrate. Maybe we can actually leave that person or maybe just see them from time to time, so to feel better about ourselves for finally taking a stand. Whatever we do, however we choose, we do it with love . . . love for ourselves that is the secret, **the key to the new YOU.**

So now we have grown, amazing wisdom is born within us. We have existed in this human condition an entire life span and finally somehow we just know "it is not about what they can do for us, it is only and has always been only, about what we can do for them".

It does not make anything any better or easier, it certainly and for sure, does not change their behavior or ability to treat us any nicer or even any different than they have ever treated us, somehow though that doesn't matter anymore; we are just a changed person.

Amazing grace has touched us, unfortunately through our own struggle, through our toughest difficulties and all we can do is treat them better . . . no matter what or how they are to us, that is the only thing we will and can do now.

And somehow, some magical way when we perform these simple task these most miniscule life lessons that are in all actuality larger than life character adjustments... greatness happens for us!

Yes it also begins in increments, yet good things only wonderful and clean and genuine things, begin to happen to . . . and for us. And even yet again somehow some incidental way we don't even know that it is not because we are looking for the better things to occur or that we hope for health wealth and happiness . . . yet, oh so suddenly, we don't even realize and are not actually even aware, that it is not because we want . . . but that we have earned small rewards and only goodness and greatness are ours, for all the days of the rest of our lives.

And then as if that is not enough, yet a new character value is born somewhere in us. How we begin to look at what is good and great is so vastly different, from how we used to think of these things.

In former days we needed mega bucks to think it was a good or great thing and now all we need is genuine kindness and love to fill a happy heart and we are glowing . . . and again . . . and still, if that cannot be done for us we can and simply will do it, for ourselves!

Oh yes, for no other reason than that **kindness, that love, is already within us.** And nobody can or will ever make us feel any better than **we can already feel all on our own.**

🦋 I think when we are with people we love and we are watching them struggle and we can even see they are hyper and anxious and things feel chaotic, we surely don't mean to fall into that trap, yet pretty soon . . . we are acting like them.

So when everything is a mess around you, and the people you are closest with, are going through hell or difficult times to say the least . . . knowing now what we know, how can we avoid stepping into their negative energy and still be a light in their life to assist them in kindness as they make their way through this battlefield we live in?

If ever there has been any one thing I have learned in my times of heartache and or difficulty, I guess I could easily sum it up for you in just one simple word . . . **detachment.** Yes, that would be it. It is a tool readily available for us that changes our pathway and brings us to peace, even in our most tumultuous times.

I have come to know in this human experience we move through night by night, day by day, that there are only two ways we deal with anything that comes toward us. We have heard it and read it so many times. Your situation is either positive or negative, or our emotions are either filled with love or fear. Life is up or it is down, you are in, or you are out . . . I can say it a hundred different ways, however, I do not care how you cut it . . . we can either get in their mess and wallow with them or . . . detach, simply detach for a greater peace. I choose peace. And what is most special about detachment is you can do this with anything.

Detachment is clearly an **ability to let go.** So simple yet so difficult to accomplish in times when you desperately want to control your outcome . . . oh and this is the best . . . every one else's too!

So how do we incorporate detachment in a world of dysfunction? Well, when the thoughts come into our head to fret and worry, scream and cry, we begin to redirect what is going on in our minds. This could consist of a simple silent movement of our breath if you are capable of staying focused, if not a more powerful objectivity will be a GOD send. I want to add in tough situations TV or even reading is usually not an option, but a more mind provoking task like maybe a puzzle that drives you nuts if you can't seem to fit all those pieces back where they belong. My preference was "Unscramble the words" it always filled my brain **and my reward was peace** almost every single time. Try it and discover the simplicity for yourself.

Ok, so we have thrown out plenty of cues. What is the answer? What is the message I am trying so desperately to convey, when I say you are the miracle, when I imply you know it all? How can I make you hear me and how can I convince you to trust that my words are truth? How can I get you to understand that you have the power of all things... within you . . .

I want to introduce you to the simple greatest tool, in helping you to open your heart and mind to whom and what you really are. I want you to become acquainted with the single element that will change your life. This powerful yet easy advantage can and will set you free.

You have seen it everywhere. You have heard it talked about. So why would you have thought it hogwash before and consider testing it now? Surely not because I am telling you to try it. Really, what would make what I am implying any more suggestive to you, than what you have seen or read before?

Well, if you are following my material then you are probably one of the many people suffering some sort of dilemma or crisis right now. Perhaps it is not you, but someone close to you and my words are being passed along. The suffering person, many times, needs to fall all the way to the lower level, to decide to try something new. Their nose usually has to hit the cement and it is generally right about then that they realize GOD and the tools he has provided within us, really do in fact work. So when your face hits the stone, I hope the boulder you fall on, has these very words on it.

Meditation is for sure the single **simple tool** that will **change your life!** It does not matter if you are injured, sick, broke or even broken hearted, meditation will in fact bring you closer to your higher power and in doing so, you will begin to create the life you truly deserve.

I hope to introduce helpful steps and simple techniques on how and when to begin in the days ahead.

🦋 So . . . why meditation? What makes this simple tool so powerful? Well the quandary of understanding the mind, in spite of sages and seers, through time and toil, in spite of technology and know how, the brain in all its miraculous ability, undoubtedly remains a puzzle at the very core of our essence.

It is said that the average mind has some sixty thousand thoughts a day. Most generally speaking, it is also stated that we tend to have the same sixty thousand thoughts, over and over in our average day to day existence.

We have learned and are trained to live in a state of worry, to not accept the influence we have available within our very selves. We have acquired an ability to not trust the very power we are equipped with to fully serve our every need. It would be like putting gasoline in our vehicle, if we would only reach inside ourselves, to grab the pump and fuel the cab!

So if we carve away all the fanciful explanation, if we elect bare bones descriptive and choose an uncomplicated approach, in meditation the simple task is silence, which is all we need do for peace and positive change . . . only to quiet the mind.

Daniel Coleman clearly states in his forward produced for Yongey Mingyur Rinpoche on "The Joy of Living" that Rinpoche acting as an expert practitioner in alliance with Richard Davidson, the director of the Waisman Laboratory for Brain Imaging and Behavior at the University of Wisconsin writes… "For example, systematic training in meditation when sustained steadily over years can enhance the human capacity for positive changes in brain activity to an extent undreamed of in modern cognitive neuroscience".

And please allow me to reiterate the two simple words in laymen terms that need only to jump out at you in this informative statement I recognize, admire and present to you clearly are… "**undreamed of.**" Yes that's how powerful a tool meditation really will be, even in a mind not ready and unprepared to make positive changes, yet nonetheless, positive changes can and will take shape in the most novice experience of a simple **silencing of the mind.**

So, once again we recognize the query . . .

What is meditation and why meditate? Meditation is a powerful yet unexplainable silence you can only come into in the presence of GOD. One might ask how you can make such a statement.

Sages and seers, doctors and even quantum scientists will surely all have a more than unusual and different explanation of the simple, however, persuasive task. No two will agree, nor denote comparable mention of such.

I like to say it is the untouched essence of a spirit that resides somewhere between your soul and your sacred self, an eternity that stretches from your core to the very core of the Universe vast and wide like a rope that binds you to a power you cannot touch or see or feel . . . yet somehow, someway it is you and you know it even in your smaller mind, the mind you function with everyday that allows you to frolic through this physicality.

Now, I know that sounds like a lot. For even some of you it may very well be too deep, or perhaps, too much. Break it apart though and you will come to understand, simply stated, it is quietness so still it cannot be shared and in such solitude you can only be with **GOD**. **The God that is in you and no question, the GOD that is you.**

I believe this is the state you lie in; in the womb of the women you unknowingly would come to share a lifetime with, a bond so strong she would allow you to live in her body! Here you experience a peacefulness untouched from humanness . . . and the only other most possibility of such . . . is in the traveled spaciousness of meditation.

So, is there a greater peacefulness than the **untouched silence** . . . that **simple moment** you *share with GOD* . . .? Unequivocally not!

"You can hear the footsteps of GOD when silence reigns in the mind."

Sri Sathya Sai Baba

🦋 I can tell you one thing for sure; I am not a guru, a sage, or a seer. I have no special ability that allows me to speak or teach of such a significant material. This writing or any of the script set forth over many weeks, that I have been allowed to produce for your reading pleasure, or more appropriately, awareness, came through me, not from me.

I can remember opening the pages to Neil Donald Walsh "Conversations with GOD" book one, book two and book three and reading that his writing did not come from him but through him. "Quite a statement" I thought, however, something strange happened next that allowed me to realize his expressions were truth.

I was reading his material, but they were my words! They were my thoughts on his pages, yes, but how? As if a light went on in my head . . . **I knew readily we were one**, all humans just one . . . acting as many. So as this writing began to come through me, surely, I felt that if I questioned Mr. Walsh . . . then why would anyone, not question me?

Well I can only share the moment and yes it is coming through me, not from me . . . and for this most powerful gift, I am grateful. So how or why I would be chosen to deliver such a work . . . is far beyond my comprehension.

Please allow me though, to suggest a simple technique for meditation; sharing only, that as we are silent, so too are we one with **GOD** . . . *And* based on what I have just expressed to you, if you are looking for a more formal training there are plenty of publications available, even some I have mentioned previously in my communication. You might also choose to seek out the material featured on the subject, at any of your favorite book stores and/or libraries.

With that said, we will discuss some of the things I like to do before I meditate in the pages ahead . . . *And* may I remind you "this is all for you to accept or reject" I only offer a suggestion . . . nothing more and nothing less.

"The superior man thinks always of virtue the common man thinks of comfort."

Confucius

My simple steps to meditation begin with comfort. I would suggest you go to the most calming area of your living space. Of course, there will be times when you are out in nature, perhaps under a tree, or walking by the water, or even just out for a casual stroll and you can quiet the mind and focus on the inhale and exhale of your breath. This will bring you into a softer meditative state and allow you to continue on with your walk or whatever it is you are doing at the time, and yet feel quiet refreshed when the mind resumes its normal heavy thinking load.

However, for a day to day practice, find that comfortable space. For me it is a favored chair in my bedroom that helps to relax my high A personality. It is an ideal fit that allows my back to be perfectly straight, my feet flat on the floor, my hands positioned so that they rest comfortably in my lap, open with palms up and one lying on the other or thumbs lightly touching index fingers and again, with palms up. Ok, there have been times when I have sat on the floor or laid on the couch simply in a soothing position, the key though is to establish a pattern and follow it from day to day. This will assist the mind in recognition of the practice and it will bring you into a quieter state, most times, quicker and easier. I want to add, that I prefer to meditate in the early hours of the day, you can choose your own space and time, so long as it makes you feel good!

I also like the morning time as I am fresh out of bed, the house is peaceful and quiet and in that space, I find I am within myself. This allows a softer transition as I begin my practice. Now let me interject, if life is dealing a blow and I am having a chaotic morning, I might just wait till later in the day.

Assuming you have established your meditation space and have qualified a comfortable place to begin, I will provide four quick and easy steps that will help to expedite the peacefulness required to prompt your practice. They will be made available in this script as we proceed.

"So ring the bells that still can ring forget your perfect offering, there is a crack in everything that's how the light comes in."

Rumi

🦋 The light of GOD is rapture. It will caress you and soothe you; it will fill you with a peacefulness one cannot even imagine in our human comprehension. Feel it, focus on it and it will touch your core . . . Step one in my meditation is the light. Visualize a brilliant white light above the top of your head. You might see pure white sunrays beaming down upon you. If this feels difficult, and remember it does take practice to learn your routine, you can picture anything white. It is whatever works for you. I am awed by the sky and as a result I will vision the clouds and see that white luminescent light coming into the very crown of my skull. I will then focus hard on that light and let it touch every part of my body from my head to my toes. I allow it to soften and soothe me, till I cannot express the quietness that fills my being.

Step two in my meditation is a mantra. It is said that the mind cannot employ two thoughts at the very same time. We all know just from thinking, this is so true. A mantra is just a word, one simple word repeated over and over, the purpose is to block out any other thoughts so the mind can be silent and in silence you will find peace and in peace, there is **GOD**. You would want to pick a calming word, as words have a great effect on our brain. I use the word **GOD** just to remind myself that my meditation is my time with a higher power, the power I can only touch in silence.

Step three in my meditation is to bring my attention to the area between my eyebrows. Sounds odd, but its not hard. Simply set your concentration on that space right there between your brows. This is your third eye, the eye that can see without your eyes. We have all heard people say, they use the eyes in back of their head. This will open your mind to all the wonder of your universe and it is amazing once you learn this simple technique, it will change your life and open doors for you, you never thought possible!

Step four in my meditation is breathing. Give thought to your breath and you must know there is **GOD**. After all, our breath is there for us anytime and all the time, and as much of it as we want. It's just an endless supply . . . *and without it, you are dead*. Focus on your breath, slow and easy, in through the nose and out through the mouth, over and over. With soft and gentle repetitious breathing you are instantly peaceful, ever so peaceful. Enjoy it. This is trial and error at first, yet with repeated practice you only get better and better. If you can get yourself to fifteen minutes a day you will be great . . . **I promise.**

"A wise man should have money in his head, but not in his heart."

Jonathan Swift

I would be sure that many people would assume that I must have money now to support my statements of being successful, and yes having money is a wonderful thing and I have a fine feeling I will always acquire more than a goodly amount of it, however, that is not how I measure success.

I measure my success by the tender most feeling in my heart. I measure my success by the calmness and love that I have in my soul for myself and for all of the humans that encompass this vast universe, in spite, of their shortcomings and dysfunction and most of all . . . in spite, of what they might have done to me.

I measure my success in knowing now . . . That I have the ability to do and have and be whatever I want. Yes, this is true and while I admire Ronda Byrnes for her thought provoking work in "The Secret" and suggest you read the book, no, my having said this did not come from that directive.

In as much as I do follow a similar creed and surely have experienced a great deal of what they proclaim, early on in my life, and for sure "**As you think so shall you be**" we must never forget, these words come from a source whose transcript has left a reflection for thousands of years!

His name is **"Jesus" and his book is the "Bible."** And for all of you folks out there that might not have liked that I have said this, just know that there are no mistakes and just as I have explained for you early on in this writing, how those puzzle pieces are put perfectly in place **through a power far greater than yourself**, please understand that this "Jesus" the one who took the beating, came from that very same intelligence . . . that so carefully placed you and I… **right where we belong!**

So, is money good? Yes for sure. If you are positive, will it help you to get it? Yes for sure. Is that what this writing is about? **Absolutely not.**

🕊 Opening with a continuum of our last dialogue on why crisis, catastrophe, and or calamity again, however you choose to label, literally reinvents itself in different ways forcing our abilities to move in a direction necessary for us to fulfill our fondest dreams.

If you continually pursue what will bring you cash the quickest way . . . and we all do and not because we want to, but that we really believe we must . . . to acquire the money we really do need to survive, much less, just to live and enjoy life. As a result, our soul the very essence of our spirit must and will change our direction and does so only to move us toward our truest hearts desire, as humorous and unbelievable as this sounds.

It is a critical step in our growth once again, that we understand this mechanism. Yes, till we begin to know and appreciate that we are here right now in this moment . . . the only moment there really is, to achieve our grandest desire, our greatest goal, and to also realize that, that is exactly what we were genuinely placed here to do . . . life, our very existence will continue to be in total chaos.

Our soul will actually work harder to bring us to our greatest, grandest vision, allowing us to perform the duty we were actually placed here to accomplish, and in that, if truth be told, we finally recognize who and what we really are. Thus, until we achieve our successes it is, in fact, a very scary roller coaster ride . . . So buckle up and take a seat with GOD!

Now do you sit there blaming yourself for taking all the wrong roads and walking all the wrong tracks? Do you wonder more than not, why it seems just when you think you are finally in the right place, you just seem to hit a dead end and life just brings you, to yet, another screeching halt! Remember I have told you it is a perfectly planned program woven and designed with a tapestry sewn just for you. You will, in fact, take all the right roads, simply because there are no wrong roads.

This is your creation designated through a power far greater than yourself. That power marks your step, creates each new beginning and every single stride along the way and when you are stopped from what you think is a great loss in your life, it is only because each experience is of a significant measure and the more you learn . . . the greater you grow... and when time is perfect, so perfect nothing can or will stop you, *the GOD that is in you and is you* . . . will then allow you to achieve your grandest and even greater aspirations, more . . . far more, **than one can ever come to imagine!**

Ok, so lets talk about confidence. Confidence is a wonderful thing, for sure it is something we all want; getting it though and then keeping it, many times is truly life challenging. Does it take a special strength to acquire this monumental ability? Well, lets examine the thought.

I use the people that are out there promoting their story. They have done something great and imply, this is how we get to build our confidence. Understand I am genuinely proud and awed of the great accomplishments some of our fellow human beings demonstrate. However, building confidence is a personal opportunity . . . and its all up to you!

I might add as I have stated in previous writings "when we struggle we grow". Your growth is your power and when you are growing you are building a strength that goes unnoticed in common reality. You do not have to climb a mountain. You do not have to march one hundred thousand miles alone, with a backpack on your shoulders. You do not have to walk a tight rope from the top of one sky scraper, to another.

Your mountain is happening minute by minute, hour by hour. Your struggles are all around you day by day. They are in your lack of money when it is necessary to feed your family. They are in your bones when you are racked with disease. They are in your heart when the love of your life has left you on the door step alone . . .and you must go on, it is a simple quest for survival. Yes, will this build confidence . . . Yes, you bet it will and does!

How we acquire this confidence though, is totally up to us. Remember we are chosen for the task set before us . . . When we are caught in the Power, there is no magic, we will do all that has been set forth in our prescribed experience and, most times, we will fight every step of the way.

And yes this also will and does build confidence . . . We will notice how hard we have worked. We will notice how many tears we have cried along the way. We will thank GOD when the sun finally shines and we can breathe with peace. We will suddenly start to notice a specific difference, something most unlike ourselves, a feeling we have never quite known in our lives. We have struggled, yet still pushed through it. Now we stand a little taller, we feel a little lighter . . . We realize we are proud of the difficult time we have most recently experienced and how well we have, indeed, handled our self through it all and in that . . . we are awed with the confidence we have simply earned from it! This can only happen through our power and that power is and always has . . .**only been GOD.**

I began to realize as life changed . . . so too would I. I would be different . . . I would be new and all too soon, I also began to know, in the final step . . . none of it would matter.

All the people, all the heartache, all the struggle would not be there and it never really was there at all. Yes, in that last moment of my breath there would only be . . . me and GOD. *And* in quiet reflection I would also come to understand that it has always and only been . . . ***me and GOD.***

It seems we must tread full circle to get to this place, never really understanding why or what any of it truly means at all. Somehow though, in the shadow of our experiences we just learn to accept our knocks and blows and simply continue to elect whatever destiny sets in our flight plan!

Yet, a beautiful existence ensues as difficult as it unquestionably is and life all in its legendary wonder evolves . . . we are caught right smack in the middle of it all and never even ask why.

So is there reason . . . well no. Can there be justifiable cause . . . not hardly. Are you the winner or the loser . . . can't say? Is there even a beginning and an end . . . who really knows.

However, I have come to close terms with this discovery and you can simply accept or reject this requirement. Our opportunity though . . . is to work it! *And* that means you can in fact . . . read it, think it, walk it, run it . . . jump it . . . if that's what you need to do! How you arrive at your final destination is up to you . . . *and your power* . . . will run that course with you. *I call that power GOD . . .*

🕊 In the case of Faith . . .

Yes, we even question our faith. Although we know somewhere in the tiny crevices of our minds, in a universe overflowing with chaos . . . we are sure of only one thing. Everything passes but GOD.

However, we live in the illusion that something greater, that mystical, magical, unseen thing that stands amidst all that we are and all that we know must be our creator; that this entity could only be the inventor, the actual architect of our reality and must be able to fix anything, at any time and this unquestionably . . . we call faith.

So we stand in the middle of a GOD that does not give us a break. A GOD that does not lessen our grief, but . . . that some incredible, unpredictable even unimaginable way, we undeniably know that it gives us the courage to somehow get through it, and again indisputably . . . we call this faith!

So what's going on with our GOD? Why is he making it so tough? Why can't the miracle, the provision from our almighty deity be in peace . . . ? Why the constant suffering? Why do we have to experience the nightmare, to come into the wisdom of our own spirituality? Who can answer, who can really say?

Could not GOD, the infamous magic of it all, make it somewhat easier on us and does this as it is, create a resentment toward the divinity we so desperately search for?

Well, of course it does, and again that is the remarkable power of the universe to work in extraordinary ways!

Yet a heart in despair will lean on the intelligence of a thing we cannot solidify in any reality, and never give up, or never give in, but only know that somehow in some numinous way . . . that grace, that essence, will in fact provide exactly what we need, and it does . . . and this, once again . . . can only and forever . . . be our faith.

> **"When you are caught in the Power,
> the only thing you can do is keep the faith"**
>
> **Donna DiMarco ***

∞

I must encourage you to read "About the Author" in the following pages. It is a powerful presentation of how divinity actually plays out in our present day realities. It allowed me to realize the necessity in sharing some of my story with all of you.

I am still so very awed at how this correspondence came through me, even when I was writing about myself . . . that feeling of dictation remained.

And so I take this opportunity to be certain that you will enjoy this material right to the very last page.

And always and forever, thank you.

About the Author

These are just a few of the interesting facts that guided me through a most difficult time in my life. In deep and quiet reflection I will share some of them with all of you.

The Green Glass Building

It was just one of those days, I could feel the anxiety race through my body like the engine of a freight train pulling a hundred cars. I would enter this building on this particular day, only because the Internal Revenue Service was neatly housed inside of it.

Every single time I entered this structure I would have the very same reaction. My nerves were rattled. It seemed there were few things I could not tolerate doing, through my career years. Allow me to mention the circumstances though, that always seemed to punch me right in the gut!

First of all, sitting with my bankers when I was borrowing money then, any serious auditing with my accountants and God only knows lastly . . . the Internal Revenue Service. Somehow, I would get through these periods, however, it was never easy, to say the least.

It was the first time I was to enter this building and every time I did so there after, a certain feeling would come over me. I would be awestruck. I would actually have to stand back and look up to view the crystal clear and clean green glass, that would almost shimmer as the sun sparkled upon it, at different angles.

As I approached, my thoughts were always the same. I would slowly begin my stride through the entry way and peer through all the windows of all the offices, that allowed so many employees a good job and a way to make money.

"These people had to be very smart to have these positions," I would think. I was certain they were all well educated and had gone to only the best schools, unlike myself. My teaching was the school of life.

So every time I entered, it was always the very same thought... and envy mixed with heart ache would come over me . "I would love to work in this building and be normal like these people." However, I knew that was all but impossible. I also knew I was just not smart enough... and having already become the owner of DiMarco's Restaurant, the "lady boss" so to speak, would put a bandage on my greatest insecurities, that I continued to carry... through a lifetime.

The House

How could this be happening to me? It was all beyond my comprehension, but it was indeed happening and as hard as I tried, I could not stop it. I was loosing everything. I was in foreclosure and I had to get out of my home. Why? I had worked hard all of my life. Why did I lock that door? I knew deep within me it was never about money. I knew it was a series of life issues . . . from very early on . . . that would haunt me and I also knew that the only hope to fix it or find peace . . . was to find myself. Alone and broken I made my way.

How in the hell was I going to find a place to live with no job and no money, what in the world would I do? The months had all passed and it was time to get out, and of course, winter was upon us . . . to make it all a little bit harder!

It was the day . . . that would show me my direction. I was racing through my subdivision with Samantha, my dog, that I loved with my heart and soul. Sitting in the front seat next to me she was all I had . . . and she meant everything to me. I was tired and weak from it all.

I was driving passed the lovely homes in my subdivision that I had recognized so well because I had lived there for so many years. Taking in the late autumn days that seemed too soon, to be inviting winter and gazing at the already bare branches . . . something moved me.

It was one of those feelings that arise within us and we don't know quite why, but that it gave me a nudge . . . and I moved my head to look at the leaves that had fallen and were still all over the ground.

There it was right in the center of them all, so small, I drove right passed it. Suddenly I realized what I did. Immediately I stopped dead and put the car in reverse, I drove a couple of feet backward to the leaves that seemed to almost form a pile.

The tiny sign read "2 and 3 bedrooms for Rent." My nerves were rattled and as anxious as I was, I fished through my purse and found a pen and scrape of paper. Quickly I jotted the number, thinking "what are you doing you have no money." I had called on all kinds of places but they were all dead ends because of my situation . . . The fall from . . . lady entrepreneur to desperate!

"C mon Sam, we're going home and mama is gonna make a call."

I found the place easily enough and it rather surprised me, I can get lost more than I care to admit. It was almost across the street from my own subdivision and this area was still somewhat better than average. They were attractive buildings paired with lovely ponds and lots of trees, that actually enhanced the properties.

I wished it could be possible for me to live there, even though I knew it was not. They were all town homes and all I could think was . . . "Why am I wasting my time?"

I left Sam in the car and rang the bell. After a quick introduction he invited me in. I guessed him to be about 45 years old or close to it. He seemed to be a firm man, not a warm personality and definitely looking to make a deal . . . and do it quick.

The place was lovely. I walked through all the rooms and began to cry . . . tears I could not stop. He was not moved.

Sign a three year lease, I know who you are. Don't worry about money . . . It was November and he gave me till January to come up with my rent. "$1395.00 a month" he said, as I was signing . . . and thought to myself, "I must be nuts!"

I was there 3 years and never missed a beat with my rent. I was put out . . . as rapidly as I was put in . . . when the IRS froze everything I had . . .

The Call

I was standing in my kitchen of my still lovely home that I had been packing up to leave. With tears on my heart, I was preparing to move into the town home I rented with no money and no job.

Standing at my counter and dialing frantically, hoping to find a way to make money, I accidentally dialed a wrong number.

The man on the other end of the line clearly stated his name and his company and not paying attention, I did not hear a word he said. Now in a firm voice he is saying "Hello, hello are you there?" "Who is this?" I asked somewhat startled. He begins to speak and states his name again, and quickly I retort "Listen I accidentally dialed your number, I apologize" and try to hang up . . . he stops me. "Wait a minute, what's your name?" "My name is Donna and I have to go." I try to hang up and he stops me again. Finally I am firm as I state "You know, I am really sorry but I must hang up now," and still he stops me one more time . . .

Now, I am thinking maybe I am suppose to speak to this guy! He says "Who were you calling?" "I don't even know." "I like your voice, were you looking for a job?" "No, but I could have been." "Well if you want a job, I have a job." Now, I was chuckling on the phone . . . and so was he. He tells me about his mortgage company and I respond. "I don't know what I could possibly do there."

Even though, I feel I am not a fit for his position and definitely just not smart enough, he convinces me to go in and meet him . . . and I do.

I am driving now to the destination to meet the man I spoke with on the telephone. I guess I am going for an interview. I look down to read the small note I am holding in my hand . . . One Hawthorn Place . . . Suddenly, this address seems familiar to me.

I enter the parking lot. I park the car and get out of my seat to stand up . . . and I am taken aback. I am actually gasping as I look up. *Wow, wow . . . I am going for an interview to work . . . in the "Green Glass Building!"*

A Wrong Turn

I had worked at the mortgage company for three years. I came and went through the doors of the "Green Glass Building" and it was surely helping to build my confidence.

I knew even though I was living the life of hard knocks . . . I still had a potential. I could accomplish what must be done to survive . . . and make my way.

I held a pretty nice position there, I was to head their marketing team. They treated me with great respect. As it turned out, I was actually the whole marketing team. The mortgage industry was falling and people were suffering from it, that included me . . . the day I was let go.

I was watching people loose their jobs everyday and they kept me as long as they possibly could. They were wonderful to me and I was grateful for everything I shared in my time with all of them, nonetheless, I was leaving . . . what would I do?

I was driving home in despair, how much more could I take? Once again, no job, no money and the IRS taking almost everything I had . . . and yet again . . . I needed to find a place to live. My time in my townhouse was coming to an end and my thoughts were blurred . . . when I realized . . . I had made a wrong turn.

Where the hell was I? I knew I was not far from home but I felt confused, I was locked in a ton of construction, along with all the other traffic. Scrambling to get through and as dusk was turning into darkness, *so help me God as I write these words I was in my car but I was off the ground . . . It was like something grabbed me by the back of the neck and made me look up . . . the huge sign said "The Daily Herald." It was as if something, somehow was sending a message to my mind . . . and I knew . . . what I was to do.*

I found my way and made it home safe, and right then, right there . . . this writing you are reading was born . . . *Divine Order was dropping crumbs along the way and I was following my path . . . in spite of my discomfort!*

Recalling this memory for all of you, in my dimly lit bedroom, sitting at my desk . . .

I cry.

A Gracious Lady

In my townhouse clicking away on my keyboard, I am suppose to be frantic, my nerves should be at their wits end; instead I am feverishly writing. I care about nothing, only the words that fill the paper before my eyes . . . click, click, click! I cannot stop.

I love it, I love it. I am writing and somehow I am changing and I love what I am doing. I am a writer . . . me, all by myself . . . I am a writer.

I am different, I feel it in the deepest part of who I am. All the fanciful material things that meant so much before . . . big homes, big cars, big business, mean nothing to me now. Only peace is what I crave. My time with God . . . and my time with myself . . . would fill me.

However, reality once again would call my hand. Yet there would be more to endure, I must find a place to live, a job to feed Sam and I and Louie, my little kitty I picked up off the street, after he had been hit by a car.

Sam was getting old and she was failing. How would I get on without her? Everyday I would say "Sammy hang on for mama, just a little longer." I felt like I could not bare all this grief and loose her too. Sam was a German Short hair Pointer, she was liver colored so people always thought she was a black lab. She died while we were still in the townhouse. I wept and wrote. That was all I could do.

And then by chance a gracious woman came into my life and saved my tail. It was a summer afternoon, I should be out looking for apartments, but I had almost given up, and so I just keep writing.

At my desk clicking on my keyboard, the phone rings. Its my oldest son. He says, "Mom I want you to look something up for me" I said "What?" Again he speaks "Just a house." He knows I am loosing this place, but does not bring it up.

So, I turn on the internet to find this address for him and in doing so, I notice this tiny picture of an apartment complex. I quickly gave him what he wanted and went back to study the info under the photo. It has my curiosity because, I am sure there cannot be a complex where this address says it is. I can't help myself and dial the number.

The lady answers the phone. She appropriately states the title of the complex and her name. I do not offer any information, I simply say "I am curious about your address because, I am certain there are no apartments where this location claims there is."

"Well I am sorry but your wrong" she says. "No, no, there cannot be" . . . I live two minutes from there. I pass there all the time and do not see a complex" I say. "Well, there is, why don't you come over" she retorts and "What is your name?" "My name is Donna and I am not coming over there" I reply. "Do you need an apartment?" she ask. "Well, actually I do"

I respond, as the conversation continues "Then just come here and let me help you."

"You cannot help me," I say, as I am breathing anxiously and she notices it. She begins again "Listen Donna please, just drive here because you never know what I can do."

She convinces me, even though I really know there is nothing anyone can do, and where I will actually land is still a mystery. I jump in my car and I am on my way! The place is literally all of eight minutes from my house and that was only because of street lights.

I drive in and to my amazement this complex is quite lovely. They were very attractive buildings that almost reminded me of privately owned condominiums as opposed to apartments. The grounds were wooded and dressed with lovely trees, white clean sidewalks and a forest area that all but draped the entire scope. I was awed.

I knew I should not have come here because I would only be so disappointed to hear the words again, "Sorry we just can't help you."

It also had great amenities, a lovely club house, weight rooms, a very accommodating gym and an unbelievably stunning swimming pool.

Everything anyone would want and there was just no way for me to do this . . . with no money and no job! I had not even entered the building and was already feeling gloomy.

I parked the car went up the side ramp and entered the office. There she stood ready to shake my hand. She was a woman of color and I immediately sensed a genuineness about her. She was very well dressed and I could see she was a professional business woman and somehow, right in that moment . . . we struck a bond together.

It made me think of the guy unknown to me, I was going to meet at the mortgage company. We too had an instant connection. Both of these new acquaintances came out of phone numbers I had not even realized, I was to call. Yes, it was starting to feel strange like these things were planned for me . . . *I had not realized yet, that they actually were!*

After a quick introduction face to face, she says to me, "C'mon let's take a walk, I want to show you a place and you can tell me your story on the way." And Lord knows . . . I did.

Inside the tiny little apartment now, tears wet my face, falling literally off my cheek bones and sobs to match the moment . . . an uncontrollable emotion comes over me and I don't want to be embarrassed yet, I cannot help myself. This place would be so perfect for me and there was no chance of getting it!

I wonder into the bathroom and she follows me. She wants to hug me, to help me through my tears. She feels my pain and I know it. Suddenly, she turns me to face her and says "Do you want this place?" Crying hard my response was, "If only it were possible."

In a quick flash this woman I don't even know, took both my hands and cradled them in hers and began to pray softly, her words filled the room like whispers from heaven.

When she was done she held me for a moment and then took me by the shoulders and looked me right in the eyes and said "Girl, you are going to be ok."

"You told me you worked at the mortgage company three years, right? So I am guessing you have three years of pay stubs" were her exact words. My response was easy "Yes I did and I do." She then told me it would be $860.00 a month and I was thrilled . . .

Could this really be happening. It was so tiny but I loved it, I would tuck myself in there and write . . . and that is precisely what I did!

Her last words when we left that apartment were "Keep your mouth shut, let me work on this . . . and go find a job."

Diamonds

As I look back over the years I can still see this scene in my minds eye . . . I would be racing through the mall and in those days, I only shopped in the biggest and the best.

It did not matter how many times I passed a jewelry store, every single time that I did . . . a particular thought would dance through my head. "Well, if I am no longer in the restaurant business, this would be the perfect thing to do . . . I should be a jewelry person."

The stores were always so meticulously clean and all of the people that worked there were always so impeccably dressed. And then I would think to myself. "I would fit right in."

Of course, I knew that would never happen. I did not know anything at all about jewelry and for sure I knew, I could never be smart enough to hold that type of position.

As the years passed I would be racing through the malls to buy the things I needed, and my commercials would be playing over my head. When I locked the door on DiMarco's Restaurant I had five commercials on the air. I had done well over fifteen years, made a name for myself and that was all fine and dandy on the outside, however, on the inside I was dying.

Still I was doing big things, large grocery chains, book stores, car dealers and more were all placing my gift certificates in there bags. I had meetings with huge grocery stores about implementing my food, I even had meetings with theaters about putting my commercials on their screens.

Yet, I could not find peace in my belly, I knew somehow, I would take the fall. I also knew . . . I would bring that place down just to accommodate my ill feelings

It was deep inside of me, a broken piece and I did not know how to fix it. I knew though somehow, someway I would run from everything . . . just to find myself.

All the people that meant everything to me were gone . . . yet, I did business. My marriage was broken, my family was not really speaking to me . . . my children were distant . . . and still . . . I did business. Diligently, laboriously I worked DiMarco's restaurant and when it came right down to it, that was all I had left, and it was killing me a day at a time.

I loved the business but, I loved my people more. I felt in my heart the only way I was to rekindle with my family was to close the business and I knew, even though, I would not face the knowing . . . someday, that's what I would do . . . I also knew . . . I would have nothing . . . once I did!

I loved DiMarco's, I loved it, I loved it . . . I locked the door April 5th, 2005 . . . I left at 4:00 am with no word . . . My place dark and sullen . . . My lovely Restaurant gone . . .

I learned in my 72 years we can do a thing . . . but we can never go back. Kick, cry, scream and pray and you cannot change what you did.

In spite of the heartache, time was passing and I seemed to be handling it all.

Perhaps, I was somewhat wearing a dismal outlook but writing kept me alive. I loved it!

I also realized I was changed. So different from the girl in former days, that woman was more than gone. She left, "Donna left" with all her fanciful notions and no remorse to even speak of.

I actually felt like someone stuck me in a washing machine and hung me out to dry. I was squeaky clean and brand new and money meant nothing to me. Now only how I could help someone or do something even menial to make someone feel good, or give something away, just cause I knew somebody struggling would indeed enjoy getting the reward.

I started volunteering at the hospital, it gave me the opportunity to touch people that were so desperately in need of a shoulder. I also began leading the Recovery, Inc group meeting, in Libertyville, IL. I wanted to help mentally ill and nervous patients. I was a member for 30 years and felt Recovery saved my life, when I was a young girl and hemorrhaged from my nose and thought I was dying.

The days were passing. I was now tucked in my tiny, little, yet lovely . . . three room apartment. Peace was settling in my bones like a sacred water flowing from a Jesus rock, but I needed a job.

I was getting by on compensation thanks to the mortgage company but it was meager. I just did not have the fear any longer of starving or loosing things or even being alone. *By now I had realized, I was being directed and to be clear ... protected ... for sure!*

One day I was leaving my apartment, I cannot even recall where I was going but that I was standing in my hallway, when a very tall blonde woman was coming in. We bumped each other and she introduced herself. Maybe a 10 minute conversation uncovered that I was not working, its been many years and I don't remember our words. However, it was short and sweet and I knew she needed to talk and I let her. The new lady I had become, had time for everyone. As we finished . . . I was on my way.

Again I must take you back to the days of my restaurant. I was doing business, still the big boss and so troubled in my core. I was seeing a therapist and she suggested regression therapy. To this day it changed my beliefs.

I know there is life after life. I will not go through all of it in this writing, in spite of the fact, that it is very interesting. My experience, I am quite certain, would grab you. I remember every bit of the lives I lived in that session.

As the doctor was bringing me back into the room and while I was still in somewhat of a trance . . . she says to me, "There is something on the floor, look at it . . . what is it? Now, pick it up!"

As I am coming to . . . I am repeating the words over and over *"It's a dime. no it's a diamond. No, it's a dime, no, it's a diamond. Yes, it's sparkling so bright I could barley look at it, to pick it up . . . It is a diamond."* And I am awake. The session is over.

Now, back to where we left off. I don't know . . . was it a few days, maybe even a week or two, I had come and gone through my building more than a few times but this day was different . . . a card was taped to my door.

I quickly pulled it off, someone must have been here and I did not even know it, but who?

I turned the card over and a name and number was scribbled on it. What the heck? Who was looking for me and why? I could not help myself. It started my hunt.

I was all over Gurnee Mills but never really looked at the card close enough. I was finally giving up. I sat in a chair in the center of the mall got comfortable and looked up, *I just happened to be sitting right outside of a jewelry store.*

I turned that card over and decided to look closer . . . *and wouldn't you know the word Jewelers was right on the card . . . A shiver went through me . . . Could this be possible?*

I entered the Jewelry store and said "I am Donna DiMarco, is somebody here looking for me?" One of the ladies working there pointed a finger and said "I know who you are, you owned DiMarco's Restaurant." She was excited to say it, and I was thinking "What would they want with me?"

Just then another woman, quite suited and business appropriate comes from behind the counter. *She extends her hand to meet with mine and says "I am. That is my card you are holding. I was looking for you." Although I tried not to show it, I am stunned again!*

I have been in diamonds now for ten years. It has not been easy, however, I made a life doing it and It has carried me. I must also add . . . I am pretty good at it.

Although I have been ill most recently, I am recovering well. However, this has pulled me away from the jewelry store. When I will return, or even . . . if I will return at all . . . remains a mystery . . .

Remember though . . . writing is my deepest passion and I will continue to do so.

A final Note

I outlined these special incidents and circumstances, with the hope that all of my readers might see the coincidence wrapped in reality. There are no mistakes, our thoughts create our lives and if you just pay closer attention you will certainly begin to recognize *"Divine Order"* in your very own journey.

There are no words for me to thank all of you for reading my material. Each one of you touches my heart. If you are part of a book club or starting your own and would like to share questions and answers, or even your personal thoughts about my writing, just send a note to my e-mail with specifics and we can share our discussions via speaker phone.

God bless,
Donna

Donna and Samantha 1999

Donna DiMarco resides in Gurnee, IL and lives with her cat Joey. She also enjoys peace and pleasure with her family and spends most of her leisure time with her brothers Frank and Tony and sister Lorraine.

Made in the USA
Lexington, KY
20 June 2019